CONTINUUM CONTEMPORARIES
Also available in this series

Pat Barker's *Regeneration*, by Karin Westman
Kazuo Ishiguro's *The Remains of the Day*, by Adam Parkes
Carol Shields's *The Stone Diaries*, by Abby Werlock
J. K. Rowling's *Harry Potter Novels*, by Philip Nel
Jane Smiley's *A Thousand Acres*, by Susan Farrell
Louis De Bernieres's *Captain Corelli's Mandolin*, by Con Coroneos
Irvine Welsh's *Trainspotting*, by Robert Morace
Barbara Kingsolver's *The Poisonwood Bible*, by Linda Wagner-Martin
Donna Tartt's *The Secret History*, by Tracy Hargreaves

Forthcoming in this series

Annie Proulx's *The Shipping News*, by Aliki Varvogli
Kate Atkinson's *Behind the Scenes at the Museum*, by Emma Parker
Haruki Murakami's *The Wind-up Bird Chronicle*, by Matthew Strecher
Jonathan Coe's *What a Carve Up!*, by Pamela Thurschwell
Don DeLillo's *Underworld*, by John Duvall
Graham Swift's *Last Orders*, by Pamela Cooper
Michael Ondaatje's *The English Patient*, by John Bolland
Ian Rankin's *Black and Blue*, by Gill Plain
Bret Easton Ellis's *American Psycho*, by Julian Murphet
Cormac McCarthy's *All the Pretty Horses*, by Stephen Tatum
Iain Banks's *Complicity*, by Cairns Craig
A. S. Byatt's *Possession*, by Catherine Burgass
David Guterson's *Snow Falling on Cedars*, by Jennifer Haytock
Helen Fielding's *Bridget Jones's Diary*, by Imelda Whelehan
Sebastian Faulks's *Birdsong*, by Pat Wheeler
Hanif Kureishi's *The Buddha of Suburbia*, by Nahem Yousaf
Nick Hornby's *High Fidelity*, by Joanne Knowles
Zadie Smith's *White Teeth*, by Claire Squires
Arundhati Roy's *The God of Small Things*, by Julie Mullaney
Alan Warner's *Morvern Callar*, by Sophy Dale
Vikram Seth's *A Suitable Boy*, by Angela Atkins
Margaret Atwood's *Alias Grace*, by Gina Wisker

· **TONI MORRISON'S**

Paradise

A READER'S GUIDE

KELLY REAMES

CONTINUUM | NEW YORK | LONDON

2001

The Continuum International Publishing Group, Inc.
370 Lexington Avenue, New York, NY 10017

The Continuum International Publishing Group, Ltd.
The Tower Building, 11 York Road, London SE1 7NX

www.continuumbooks.com

Library of Congress Cataloging-in-Publication Data

Reames, Kelly Lynch.
    Toni Morrison's Paradise / Kelly Reames.
        p. cm. – (Continuum contemporaries)
    Includes bibliographical references.
    ISBN 0-8264-5319-8 (pbk. : alk. paper)
    1. Morrison, Toni. Paradise. 2. African Americans in literature.
  3. Oklahoma–In literature. I. Title. II. Series.

PS3563.08749 P3737 2001
813'.54–dc21   2001032580

ISBN 0-8264-5319-8

Contents

Toni Morrison's *Paradise*
A Reader's Guide

The Novelist

Chloe Anthony Wofford was born on February 18, 1931, in Lorain, Ohio, a relatively integrated steel town of about 30,000 people.* She was the second child of George and Ramah Willis Wofford. In addition to her older sister, Lois, to whom *Paradise* is dedicated, Morrison has two younger brothers. Both of her parents were from Southern families. Her father moved to Lorain from Georgia, while her maternal grandparents moved to Lorain after living in Alabama and in Kentucky. Her father worked as a shipyard welder and then in the steel mills in Lorain. Her mother was from a family of musicians and played piano at a movie theater. Morrison's grandfather was a violinist. Morrison remembers that her mother always sang around the house. So many of her family members were highly talented musicians who could play by ear that when she and her sister were given music lessons, she thought she was lacking in some way (Schappell).

---

*Biographical information is from the interviews listed in Section five as well as from articles and books by Harris, Kubitschek, and Peach.

In addition to music, her upbringing was filled with story-telling, and from these stories Morrison draws many of the mythical and supernatural elements in her works. She says, "As a child I was brought up on ghost stories—part of the entertainment was story-telling. Also, I grew up with people who believed it. When they would tell you stories about visions, they didn't tell them as though they were visions" (Ruas 99–100). In fact, Morrison's acceptance speech for her 1993 Nobel Prize focused on the importance of storytelling and the role of interpretation.

Morrison credits her family with preparing her to be successful. She says that she was "surrounded by people who had done extra-ordinary things under duress in order to survive" (Ruas 98). She was also inspired by her relatives' powerful personalities. "They never tucked tail," she recalls. "I felt much endowed by their tenacity. My father always took it for granted that I could do anything, and my mother and grandmother never entertained fragility or vulnerabil-ity" (Micucci 276). Her family always assumed that she would work and that she would be successful.

After graduating from high school with honors, Morrison at-tended Howard University, where she was nicknamed Toni. She ma-jored in English and minored in Classical Studies. In the summers, she traveled with the Howard University Players. She graduated with a B.A. degree in 1953 and then went to Cornell University, where, in 1955, she earned a Master's degree in English. The subject of her thesis was suicide in the novels of William Faulkner, a writer with whose work hers is often compared, and Virginia Woolf. She has taught at Texas Southern University, Howard University (where one of her students was Stokely Carmichael), the University of New York at Purchase, Yale University, Bard College, the State Univer-sity of New York at Albany, and the University of California, Berke-ley. She is currently the Robert Goheen Professor of Humanities at Princeton University, where she enjoys teaching undergraduates.

Morrison emphasizes the importance of teaching high-quality literature: "I always taught *Oedipus Rex* to all kinds of what they used to call remedial or development classes. The reason those kids are in those classes is that they're bored to death; so you can't give them boring things. You have to give them the best there is to engage them" (Schappell 122). Morrison teaches both literature and creative writing courses, although she acknowledges that she does not find teaching compatible with writing because the two disciplines require such different ways of thinking. So she does most of her writing during periods when she is not teaching.

Morrison began writing at age thirty, shortly before her six-year marriage to Harold Morrison, a Jamaican architect, ended in 1964. She maintained custody of their two sons, Harold Ford and Kevin Slade. After the divorce, Morrison returned to Lorain but soon moved to Syracuse, New York, to work as a textbook editor. In 1968, she moved to New York City, where she was a senior editor at Random House. While there, she worked on *The Black Book* and was instrumental in publishing many African-American writers including Angela Davis, Gayle Jones, Toni Cade Bambara, Muhammad Ali, Henry Dumas, and Leon Forrest.

Her first novel, *The Bluest Eye*, began as a short story she composed for a writing group at Howard University, where she was teaching at the time. She describes that beginning as "a little bit of a fluke"; she was required to bring new writing to the group (Borders.com). Morrison did not tell her colleagues at Random House that she was writing a novel because it was, for her, a private activity. She also did not seek a contract until the manuscript was completed. Published by Holt in 1970, the novel tells the story of Pecola Breedlove, a young African-American girl who, because her concept of physical beauty and its importance has been warped by the dominant white culture, is consumed by a desire to have blue eyes. Pecola is a tragic figure; raped by her father and neglected by her mother, she is filled with self-loathing. Her sense of worth as a black child is further challenged by a culture that embraces a Caucasian standard of beauty, a theme Morrison sought to address. Morrison says about this work, "I only wrote the first book because I thought it wasn't there, and I wanted to read it when I got through" (Schappell 93).

If Morrison finds the beginning of her career rather happenstance, she also describes writing as a crucial activity for her:

. . . what makes me feel as though I belong here, out in this world, is not the teacher, not the mother, not the lover but what goes on in my mind when I am writing. Then I belong here, and then all of the things that are disparate and irreconcilable can be useful. I can do the traditional things that writers say they do, which is to make order out of chaos. Even if you are reproducing the disorder, you are sovereign at that point. Struggling through the work is extremely important—more important to me than publishing it (Schappell 95).

As a single mother with a full-time job, finding time to write was difficult. Morrison says she wrote before her sons awoke, very early in the morning, a time of day she still prefers. She was also able to devote more time to writing in the summers, when her sons visited her family in Ohio. Among the strongest aspects of her novels are the complexity and authenticity of her characters. She says, "They are very carefully imagined. I feel as though I know all there is to know about them, even things I don't write—like how they part their hair" (Schappell 106). She warns, however, that characters must not be allowed to take control and adds that while writing *Song of Solomon*, she had to reign in Pilate.

Her second novel, *Sula*, was published in 1974. It was well received by critics and nominated for the National Book Award for Fiction in 1975. Excerpts were published in *Redbook*, and the novel was an alternate selection for the Book-of-the-Month Club. Morrison said she wrote it "based on this theoretically brand new idea, which was: Women should be friends with one another. And in the

community in which I grew up, there were women who would choose the company of a female friend over a man, any time. They were really 'sisters,' in that sense" (Jaffrey).

The two friends in *Sula* are Nel Wright and Sula Peace, women who respond very differently to the expectations of their community. Nel conforms to her mother's and then her husband's wishes, while Sula defies convention, thereby gaining a fearsome reputation. Morrison describes the genesis of the novel as her desire to investigate good and evil. Those concepts break down in the novel and become meaningless. As Morrison states:

I started out by thinking that one can never really define good and evil. Sometimes good looks like evil; sometimes evil looks like good—you never really know what it is. It depends on what uses you put it to. Evil is as useful as good is, although good is generally more interesting; it's more complicated. I mean, living a good life is more complicated than living an evil life (Stepto 13–14).

Sula is the defiant, rebellious, and sexually free character who leaves Bottom and whose behavior violates the mores of her community. Yet she seems to have a more authentic self than Nel, who leads the more conventional life. Morrison addresses the same concerns about good and evil with her characters in *Paradise*. Some of the characters most devoted to righteousness turn out to be the most violent, while some of the most compassionate characters lead unruly, dissipated lives. Both novels reveal the dangers of life at either extreme—following a rigid and judgmental morality or lacking discipline or a moral center.

Song of Solomon, Morrison's third novel, appeared in 1977. It was a Book-of-the-Month Club selection and won the National Book Critics' Circle Award. After its success, Morrison quit her editing job and devoted herself to writing full time. By this time, she felt comfortable calling herself a writer. She points out that women writers have typically found it more difficult than male writers to proclaim

writing as their profession because for women, doing so requires breaking traditional gender roles. The task is made more challenging if the writer, like Morrison, is a minority from a working-class background (Schappell).

Song of Solomon relates the story of Milkman Dead, a young black man born to a wealthy family, who lacks any sense of purpose in his life. He contrasts sharply with his best friend, Guitar, who is politically aware and becomes increasingly militant in his work to fight racism. By undertaking a journey to discover his family's history, Milkman gains a sense of identity. Central to the novel and to Milkman's character is the myth that some slaves could fly and that they escaped slavery by flying back to Africa.

Morrison's reputation was firmly established by the time *Tar Baby* appeared in 1981. Its publication put Morrison on the cover of *Newsweek* magazine, and it spent four months on the *New York Times* bestseller list. This fourth novel has never received the critical attention or acclaim of her other works. Set in the Caribbean, Florida, and New York City, *Tar Baby* chronicles the ill-fated romance between Jadine Childs, a light-skinned model accustomed to a luxurious, big-city life, and Son Green, who has jumped ship and hides in the house where Jadine's aunt and uncle work. Through the relationship, the novel considers conflicting ideas of community, family, and identity. The book also considers race relations through the white couple who employs Jadine's relatives.

Though the term *tar baby* has been used as a racial slur, the title of the novel refers to a children's story about a rabbit who encounters a glob of tar that looks like a baby, a tale Morrison says she found horrifying. The rabbit, angry that the tar will not talk to him, becomes stuck in it and cannot escape. Morrison says that the tar baby is Jadine and the rabbit is Son. She explains her use of these characters: "The tragedy of the situation was not that she *was* a Tar Baby, but that she wasn't. . . . She could not hold any-

thing to herself" (Ruas 102). Most of the characters in the novel are self-deluded and lack the ability to sustain meaningful, loving relationships. Only Jadine's aunt and uncle approach a realistic awareness of themselves; they have a loving partnership to which the other relationships fail to compare.

Morrison published her only short story, "Recitatif," in 1983. The title is a form of the musical term *recitative*, which is a style that mimics natural speech and is used in opera. The story is about the relationship between two women, Roberta and Twyla, who become fast friends in a shelter for girls but who go on to lead very different lives. Racial difference is initially a source of conflict between them, but the story never reveals which character is black and which is white. Morrison's experiment in narration in this story prefigures her similar experiment in *Paradise*, which does not specify which of the women at the Convent is white. Ultimately, the significant difference that causes tension between the two friends in "Recitatif," as they meet over the years, is economic, not racial. Morrison wanted to show in this story that racial terms are often used to indicate differences that are actually based on class. The story also reveals the similarity in the stereotypes black people and white people create about each other.

In 1986, Morrison's only play, *Dreaming Emmett*, which remains unpublished, was performed in Albany, New York, by the Capital Repertory Company. Commissioned by the New York State Writers Institute at the State University of New York at Albany, the play resurrects Emmett Till, a fourteen-year-old boy from Chicago who was killed in Mississippi in 1955 for being too familiar with a white woman. The murder shocked the residents of Mississippi, and many leaders—white and black—called for justice. When the story gained national attention and northerners began to criticize the South, however, many white leaders changed their opinion. The men accused of the crime, Roy Bryant and J. W. Milam, who at first could not obtain legal representation, suddenly found prominent lawyers rushing to their defense. In the play, Till contemplates revenge against his killers, who were acquitted of their crime because the defense appealed to the prejudices of the white jury.

In 1987, Morrison published *Beloved*, her most acclaimed work, which received the 1988 Pulitzer Prize for Fiction. The novel is based on the actual account of Margaret Garner, a slave convicted of killing her child. Sethe is the main character, an escaped slave who kills one of her daughters and tries to kill her two sons as they are about to be recaptured into slavery. Years later, a mysterious woman named Beloved, who seems to be that daughter, as well as the incarnation of a ghost that inhabits Sethe's house, appears. The novel examines slavery's impact on identity as well as on relationships between men and women and mothers and daughters. A haunting tale, it also provides detailed accounts of the abuse suffered by slaves that authors of slave narratives minimized for their white readers.

In 1998, the novel was adapted to film. Directed by Jonathan Demme, the movie featured Oprah Winfrey as Sethe, Danny Glover as Paul D, Thandie Newton as Beloved, and Kimberly Elise as Denver. While Morrison visited the set during filming, she was not significantly involved in the production. The film, which was true to the book, earned disappointing box-office returns and reviews. Morrison envisioned *Beloved* as the first work in a trilogy that would explore obsessive love. *Beloved* addresses mother– daughter love, *Jazz* romantic or sexual love, and *Paradise* religious love.

With *Jazz* in 1992, Morrison attempts to replicate aspects of the musical form in narrative:

I try to echo some of the basic characteristics of jazz music in that book by refusing to have a narrator or leader who knew everything and exactly how the music was going to turn out. Instead, the narrator had to listen to the characters the way Miles Davis listened while he performed with his musicians, and depending on what they did, that would affect the next solo or alteration in the music (Timehost).

Morrison points out that of all the characters' points-of-view, the narrator's is ultimately the least reliable source of information in the book. Set in 1920s Harlem, the novel recounts the relationship between lovers of much different ages. A young girl, Dorcas, is stabbed and killed by her jealous lover, Joe. Joe's wife, Violet, tries to stab Dorcas's body in its coffin. Morrison got the idea for the plot from a photograph by James Van Der Zee that appeared in his 1978 work, *The Harlem Book of the Dead*. The novel is an examination of obsessive love and romantic love and their relationship to personal identity. *Paradise*, the subject of this guide, appeared in 1998. The final work in the trilogy, it explores many of the issues of her previous novels, including identity, relationships, and community.

Morrison has also written in other genres. Her song cycle, *Honey and Rue*, was set to music by André Previn and performed by Kathleen Battle in Chicago in 1993. And in 1999, with her son Slade, she published *The Big Box*, a children's book based on a story Slade had written as a child. In the book, the characters are forced to live in a box because adults consider their behavior unruly, but the children argue eloquently for their freedom.

In addition to her fiction, Morrison has produced important scholarly works. The two most critical examine the role of race in American literature. In her 1988 essay, "Unspeakable Things Unspoken: The Afro-American Presence in American Literature," she addresses the revision of American literary canon. She argues that African-American literature needs to be perceived as an influential contribution to the development of the nation's literature and not merely an additional and marginalized subcategory of American literature, that entity which "according to conventional wisdom, is certainly not Chicano literature, or Afro-American literature, or Asian-American, or Native American, or . . . " (1, ellipsis in original). Morrison's purpose is to "address ways in which the presence of Afro-American literature and the awareness of its culture both resuscitate the study of literature in the United States and raise that study's standards" (3–4).

Similarly, in *Playing in the Dark: Whiteness and the Literary Imagination* (1992), Morrison studies the ways in which whiteness has been developed in contrast to what she calls an "Africanist" presence in canonical American literature. In that work, Morrison argues that the concept of racial difference is central to American literature and culture, though that centrality has been denied. Morrison asks:

> . . . whether the major and championed characteristics of our national literature — individualism, masculinity, social engagement versus historical isolation; acute and ambiguous moral problematics; the thematics of innocence coupled with an obsession with figurations of death and hell — are not in fact responses to a dark, abiding, signing Africanist presence. It has occurred to me that the very manner by which American literature distinguishes itself as a coherent entity exists because of this unsettled and unsettling population. Just as the formation of the nation necessitated coded language and purposeful restriction to deal with the racial disingenuousness and moral frailty at its heart, so too did the literature, whose founding characteristics extend into the twentieth century, reproduce the necessity for codes and restriction (5–6).

In *Playing in the Dark*, Morrison discusses the way that white characters and authors use black characters to define white identity. She analyzes canonical works in American literature by authors such as Willa Cather, Ernest Hemingway, Edgar Allan Poe, and William Faulkner. She thus provides a template for other literary critics, and the project she outlines has inspired many scholarly works.

In 1993, Morrison was awarded the Nobel Prize. The Nobel can be daunting, and Morrison said, "I was so happy that I had a real book idea in progress. If I hadn't, I would have thought, 'Uh-oh, can I ever write again?'" (Gray 63). The award does bring a writer a great deal of attention, good and bad. And if some critics suggested that she would not have won were she not an African-American woman, their suppositions failed to diminish her literary reputation or her popularity. Accusations that committees respond to social or political pressures follow any prize, and particularly the Nobel.

Morrison was awarded the National Book Foundation Medal for Distinguished Contribution to American Letters in 1996. In her acceptance speech, which has since been published as *The Dancing Mind*, Morrison speaks of the kind of attentiveness that reading and writing requires and how rare that type of mental discipline has become. She says:

> There is a certain kind of peace that is not merely the absence of war. It is larger than that. The peace I am thinking of is not at the mercy of history's rule, nor is it a passive surrender to the status quo. The peace I am thinking of is the dance of an open mind when it engages another equally open one—an activity that occurs most naturally, most often in the reading/writing world we live in (7).

Morrison has also edited two books of essays on controversial events that provoked heated discussions about current social problems in the United States. *Race-ing Justice, En-gendering Power: Essays on Anita Hill, Clarence Thomas, and the Construction of Social Reality*, published in 1992, addresses sexual harassment and the stereotypes evoked by the public display of African-American bodies during Thomas's televised confirmation hearing prior to his appointment to the U.S. Supreme Court. Similarly, the 1997 *Birth of a Nation'hood: Gaze, Script, and Spectacle in the O.J. Simpson Case* concerns how race, the role of the media, and the pursuit of justice in a racist society impact an African-American accused of a crime. When asked in an on-line conversation how she feels about African-Americans' current "struggle," she responded:

If you mean by that economic strides that some African Americans have made, I am very encouraged by the changes since the 60s and the increased number of professional African Americans in all walks of life, from Wall St. to the Academy, to corporations and [the] business community. If your question refers to the level of violent racism in the U.S., I am not at all optimistic. It seems as though the progress that African Americans make historically is accompanied by an equally negative response to that progress. (Timehost)

Morrison has also written several essays on immigration. Ultimately, however, Morrison's literary reputation will rest on her novels—the power of the stories she tells and the often-noted lyricism of her literary voice. While lasting literary fame is notoriously difficult to predict, Morrison's place in the literary canon of the United States seems secure.

2

The Novel

P*aradise* is the final work in what Morrison conceived of as a trilogy of novels united by a common theme—excessive or obsessive love that leads to violence. Just as *Beloved* explores maternal love and *Jazz* romantic love, *Paradise* explores religious devotion. The novel is also an investigation of a utopian community. Morrison has explained that she wanted to explore "why paradise necessitates exclusion" (Mulrine). She elaborates:

The isolation, the separateness, is always a part of any utopia. And it [the novel] was my meditation . . . and interrogation of the whole idea of paradise, the safe place, the place full of bounty, where no one can harm you. But, in addition to that, it's based on the notion of exclusivity. All paradises, all utopias are designed by who is not there, by the people who are not allowed in. (Farnsworth)

In the community she creates, religious fervor turns into condemnation of others, and the founders' obsession with protecting their town leads them to betray its principles.

Morrison's original title for the novel was *War*, but her publishers did not consider that title marketable. It is perhaps more fitting than

Paradise because the novel opens with nine men raiding a building known as the Convent to kill the women who live there. These men see their actions as righteous. They have set out to rid their town, Ruby, Oklahoma, of the evil that has infested it, and they believe—or have convinced themselves—that these women are its source. The men also feel justified because they think they are carrying out the townspeople's wishes, although we learn later that some members of the town try to prevent the attack. Though the massacre is chronologically the final event of the story, its placement at the novel's beginning creates suspense about Ruby's inhabitants, the women who live at the Convent, the relationship between these two groups, and the impetus for the opening slaughter. The first chapter also introduces many of the novel's themes: religious fervor, isolation, exclusion, and gender conflict.

The first sentence—"They shoot the white girl first"—sets up an uncertainty, one that may or may not be resolved. Critics have tried to identify various characters, including Mavis, Seneca, and Pallas, as the white woman. Such attempts miss Morrison's point, however, which is that the character's race does not matter but that we have been taught by our culture to believe that it does. She emphasizes repeatedly that knowing someone's race provides no real insight:

It was important to me to demonstrate that [concept] in *Paradise*, by withholding racial markers from a group of black women, among whom was one white woman, so that the reader knew everything, or almost everything, about the characters, their interior lives, their past, their faults, their strengths, except that one small piece of information which was their race. And [for the reader] to either care about that, like the characters, dislike them, or dismiss the characters based on the important information which was what they were really like. And if I could enforce that response in literature, it was a way of saying that race is the least important piece of information we have about another person. Forcing people to react racially to another person is to miss the whole point of humanity. (Timehost)

Morrison's strategy in making one of the Convent women white is similar to that used in her only short story, "Recitatif." Morrison has referred to the story as "an experiment in the removal of all racial codes from a narrative about two characters of different races for whom racial identity is crucial" (*Playing in the Dark* xi). She never identifies which character is black and which is white in the story, though the story itself concerns the impact of the characters' racial difference on their relationship. The racial ambiguity in the story creates a mystery that forces readers to confront their racially based expectations for characters.

Paradise reveals both group and individual histories in a circuitous fashion. We get pieces of stories, sometimes from a narrator, but often through different characters' interior monologues. The information is thus delivered to the reader out of chronological order. This narrative strategy—a nonlinear plot told by multiple narrators—is familiar to readers of Morrison's works and is one of the reasons her writing style is so often compared to William Faulkner's. This style is exemplified in the novel's first chapter, which recounts the thoughts of several of the men who search the Convent and is also used to introduce the tale of the building's history. Because the characters all interpret events in their own way and even the narrator may not be reliable, we must always consider from whose point-of-view we are receiving insight as we piece together the story and assess the characters' actions. Morrison likens her method of storytelling to the actual way we obtain information in life. She points out that readers' expectation "now more than ever for linear, chronological stories is intense because that's the way narrative is revealed in TV and movies . . . but we experience life as the present moment, the anticipation of the future, and a lot of slices of the past" (Mulrine).

The Convent

Located seventeen miles outside of Ruby, the Convent was originally an elaborate mansion. Ironically, its first owner, an embezzler, had designed it in the shape of a bullet so that it would be easy to defend were he attacked. The Sisters of the Sacred Cross later transformed the building into a missionary schoolhouse for Native American girls. Officially named Christ the King School for Native Girls, everyone called it the Convent. The nuns, offended by the mansion's sensuous decor, removed what they could practically dispose of. However, traces of the original decadence remain in the ornate fixtures and the carved marble; though the nuns "chipped away all the nymphs . . . the curves of their marble hair still strangle grape leaves and tease the fruit" (4). Brimming with sensuality but marked by renunciation, the building itself embodies contradictory motives. And its history mirrors the reasons for the raid that opens the novel, for the men most revile the deviant sexuality they attribute to the women who live there. The men try to purge the sexuality in the house just as the nuns had earlier.

After the school failed, two women remain at the Convent, the mother superior and Connie, the woman Mother had rescued as an orphan from an unspecified South American city many years before. They raise vegetables, fruit, and incredibly hot peppers, that they sell, along with pies and pepper relish, to the residents of Ruby. They also provide occasional aid or temporary refuge to women from the town. Connie cares for the aging, ill Mother, and several years before Mother's death, the first of a group of abused and traumatized women who find refuge at the Convent arrives.

To the men who invade the Convent, these women are ". . . detritus: throwaway people that sometimes blow back into the room after being swept out the door" (4). The women's blatant sexuality scandalizes the men and stirs their imaginations. The youngest of the group, K.D., experiences the attack on the Convent as if it were a dream sequence, and the colors remind him of "the clothes of an easily had woman" (4). Another man wonders how women's "plain brains [could] think up such things: revolting sex, deceit and the sly torture of children" (8). While the men lack factual support for their accusations, changes in their town have created rumors and fear and require a scapegoat. Ironically, the very men who pursue these women pride themselves on having founded a town where women were safe because "nothing for ninety miles around thought [they] were prey"(8). The recurrence of that sentiment throughout the chapter reveals the men's protective attitude toward the women of Ruby and emphasizes that those women must conform to the men's idea of virtue in order to be valued.

One of Steward's later memories indicates that women's virtue has not always been judged so harshly by the men of Haven and perhaps of Ruby. Steward's older brother, Elder, who personifies the exacting moral standards of Morgan men for his younger sibling, never forgot the fight he got into upon his return to the United States after World War I. He saw two white men argue with a black woman whose dress leads Elder to assume she is a prostitute. He at first identifies with the men. However, when they beat her, he finds himself physically defending her. When he arrives at home, he chooses to keep his tattered uniform and asks to be buried in it. His attitude toward the woman has greatly changed: "Whatever he felt about her trade, he thought about her, prayed for her till the end of his life" (94–95). He cannot forgive himself for fleeing after the fight rather than staying to help her. Steward is proud of his brother's strict personal moral code but does not relate to Elder's charitable attitude toward the woman: ". . . it unnerved him [Steward] to know [the story] was based on the defense of and prayers for a whore. He did not sympathize with the whitemen, but he could see their point, could even feel the adrenaline, imagining the fist was his own" (95). Steward's judgmental tendency and his aversion to women's sexuality undermine his own moral code.

The Founding of Ruby

As the men search the Convent for the hiding women, their thoughts reveal their opinions about the women and also their memories about the 1949 founding of the town twenty-five years earlier. Morrison employs interior monologues to establish Ruby's history. Ruby is actually the second town the families attempt to establish. The first, Haven, was founded in 1889 in Oklahoma Territory by freedmen who refused to become tenant farmers or settle for the limited opportunities available to them in the South. Initially successful, by 1934, Haven had been severely weakened by economic hardship and by 1948 was barely surviving it. After World War II, a group of men, grandsons of Haven's founders, decided to move to a new location and try again.

The first thing the men who settled Haven did was build a communal Oven. Located in the center of town, the Oven was a symbol of the settlers' achievement. It unified the townspeople, bringing them together for meals and celebrations. Before moving West, the war veterans first disassembled the Oven to take along. Intended to be a reminder of the town's history and the veterans' determination to succeed where Haven had failed, the Oven ultimately becomes a focal point of discontent and disagreement in Ruby. Young people congregate there, and the misunderstandings between the generations finally manifest as an argument about whether the Oven's inscription reads "Beware the Furrow of His Brow" or "Be the Furrow of His Brow." The Oven never provides for Ruby the unifying force it created in Haven. Even on the trip to find a new home, the women resented the space it took and the time the men spent rebuilding it in their new location.

The men remember better times in Ruby, like the horse race organized early in the town's history by a man named Ossie. The war veteran donated his Purple Heart to the winner, a seven-year-old boy called K.D., short for "Kentucky Derby." The new town, which for three years had been called New Haven, is officially renamed Ruby in honor of K.D.'s mother, who is also Steward and Deacon Morgan's sister. Ruby grew ill on the journey to the new location and died because the hospitals in Demby and Middleton did not admit blacks. A nurse in Middleton did call for help when Ruby died, but the brothers found later that she had been trying to contact a veterinarian. These circumstances increase the town's desire to become self-sufficient. Ruby's is the only death among the town's founders and their descendants until the end of the novel. The absence of death is interpreted by the townspeople as a sign of protection, but it also signifies a foreboding but unnamed covenant, a deal made, perhaps subconsciously, by the town's original settlers that may lead to their undoing. When Deek and Soane's sons are killed in Vietnam, they determine that the deal mandates that people not leave Ruby.

As the twins, Steward and Deacon Morgan, approach the cellar of the Convent they have just invaded, their thoughts about Ruby center on the reasons for its willed isolation. They are the two most powerful men in Ruby because of their ancestry, leadership, and wealth. The men sense each others' thoughts, and "between them they remember the details of everything that ever happened—things they have witnessed and things they have not" (13). Among their memories are incidents when white men came through their town and harassed young girls but were run off by Ruby's unified, intimidating men. But the people of Ruby are not isolated from white people only; all outsiders are viewed as threats. The suspicion of outsiders is a legacy from the founding of Haven.

Those Haven settlers, following enticing advertisements for Western land, were routinely shunned by whites and Native Americans. But their rejection by black towns already underway solidified their unity and purpose and made them wary of everyone else. The advertisements' slogan, "Come Prepared or Not at All" (13), a phrase

Morrison appropriated from actual advertisements of the period, signified that settlers needed to bring sufficient cash and supplies to last until the town became profitable. But when the future settlers of Haven were rejected by the blacks of Fairly, Oklahoma, some of them suspected that they were turned away not solely for monetary reasons, but because of their dark complexions. The Fairly residents' offer of food, blankets, and money deepened the insult, and that rejection comes to be known in Haven mythology as the "Disallowing." The alleged prejudice of Fairly's inhabitants represents the internalized racism that values lighter skin as well as their practical realization that those with lighter skin were more likely to be able to deal profitably with whites.

Having been turned away by the people of Fairly, the group lacked direction. Steward and Deek's grandfather, Zechariah Morgan, also known as "Big Papa," took his son Rector (later nicknamed "Big Daddy") into the woods to pray for guidance. A man appears who leads the group to what will become Haven. Only Zechariah, Rector, and, occasionally, children can see the man, but the group is convinced that God is leading them. After a year of work and negotiation, they obtain the land from the State Indians who own it. The Haven settlers' belief that they were following their destiny and were guided by God mirrors the rhetoric of American colonists who believed they were chosen by God to found a New Jerusalem. One of the cautionary tales of *Paradise* is the inherent danger when any group believes itself to be a chosen people.

The Haven men are also seduced by the promise of the American frontier: "Here freedom was a test administered by the natural world that a man had to take for himself every day. And if he passed enough tests long enough, he was king" (99). Morrison points out, however, that African-American experience of the frontier differed from both Native American and white experiences because the impetus behind the groups' moves differed greatly:

African-Americans were not immigrants in this rush to find a heaven. They had left a home. So they're seeking another home, while other people . . . were leaving a home that they didn't want to be in any longer, or couldn't be in any longer. Native Americans were being moved around in their home. African-Americans were looking for a second one and hopefully one that would be simply up to them, their own people, their own habits, their own culture, and to contain themselves in that. So it makes the motive for paradise a little bit different.

Morrison nevertheless cautions that "isolation . . . carries the seeds of its own destruction" (Farnsworth).

Mavis

The chapter titles in *Paradise* reflect the names of the women in the book. After the first chapter, "Ruby," the next four chapters tell the stories of the women who seek refuge at the Convent, though each chapter also reveals much about Ruby and its inhabitants as well. Chapter 2 narrates the story of Mavis Albright. Morrison has said that her idea for Mavis developed from "an image I had of a woman sitting on a couch that's covered in plastic, scraping potato chip crumbs away from the seams with her fingernail" (Borders.com). Mavis's chapter opens with that image, as she is being interviewed by a journalist who tries to mask her condescension with a compassionate facade. To be fair, the story Mavis tells as a photographer takes pictures of her with three of her children fails to account for her tragedy, making her seem both culpable and slow-witted. Her two youngest children have recently suffocated when she left them in a hot car. Their deaths have brought attention and interest that are foreign to her life, which in 1968, is defined by poverty and abuse.

Mavis explains to the journalist that she left the twin babies, Merle and Pearl, in the car while she shopped for wieners for her husband's dinner. Though the reporter is skeptical, Mavis insists her errand could not have taken more than five minutes. She was hurrying, not because she was worried about the babies but because of her husband Frank's anger. Part of the journalist's confusion stems from her assumption that Mavis's husband routinely comes home for dinner; she cannot understand why Mavis was so surprised by his expecting a meal. Mavis, on the other hand, cannot imagine what life would be like with a husband who came home every evening. Frank is evidently not Mavis's first husband, though he is the father of her children. The confused journalist, however, asks about Jim Albright, indicating that Jim may still be Mavis's husband according to public records. Mavis does not correct the journalist, and she later introduces herself as Mavis Albright.

Mavis's fear of Frank, who is drunk and drinking in the bathroom during the interview, makes her a somewhat sympathetic character. She braces herself as he joins her in bed that night and acquiesces to his demand for sex because she is afraid. She believes that she is being trapped and that Frank and her children plan to kill her. Whether her fear is justified or merely a paranoid delusion born of abuse by Frank is unclear. Mavis manages to escape from the house, only to realize she has nowhere to go. Typical of abusive spouses, Frank has prevented her from maintaining friendships.

She takes Frank's 1964 mint green Cadillac, which he has forbidden her to drive. For Mavis, the car is a symbol of freedom, and by stealing it from Frank she regains some power. She drives to the home of Peg but decides it is too early to awaken a woman she does not know very well. As she passes the hospital, she remembers her fifteen stays there, only four of which were for childbirth. Her recollection further establishes the extent of Frank's abuse. Finally, she drives five hours to Paterson, New Jersey, to the home of her mother, Birdie Goodroe, from whom she receives an indifferent welcome.

Birdie's attitude toward her daughter is ambivalent. Unsurprised by the escalation of violence, she reminds Mavis of her responsibility to her other children. But she also expresses her concern, reminding Mavis of what she has done for her grandchildren, and telling her, "You're all I have, now your brothers gone and got themselves shot up like—" (31). Her sons were killed in the Vietnam war, and Birdie's expressions of concern for Mavis seem more from duty than from genuine concern. She stresses her own experience rather than Mavis's. Habitually unable to maintain a focus on reality—Mavis fantasizes about living in the Cadillac during her interview and hopes to reach her mother's home in time to watch her favorite television show—Mavis thinks mainly about food as her mother questions her during dinner. But when she tells her mother that her children were trying to kill her, she encounters skepticism. Birdie tells Mavis she can stay as long as she never makes such accusations again.

When Mavis overhears part of a telephone conversation that sounds to her as if her mother is alerting Frank, she takes some money and leaves. After having the car painted, she heads for California. She offers rides to hitchhikers to supplement her gas money, and shortly after the last of these young women leaves, Mavis thinks she sees Frank and flees in terror. She runs out of gas and berates herself for her inability to plan. After spending a night in the car, she thinks of the adventurous spirits the hitchhiking women shared and decides to walk to seek help. Their example has suggested not that she should be able to take care of herself, but that she can. She walks until she sees a house through a cornfield—her destination is the Convent.

Mavis meets Connie, who cares for the aged, dying Mother. Connie immediately distinguishes herself philosophically from the people of Ruby when Mavis asks if living with just one other woman does not scare her. Connie replies, "Scary things not always outside. Most scary things is inside" (39). Ruby's leaders' inability to understand this concept contributes to the book's violent opening and conclusion.

Connie feeds Mavis, who feels secure in the kitchen. When Connie leaves her alone, Mavis finds, to her relief, that she remains at ease. She senses the presence of children in the room, including Merle and Pearl. Mavis continues to feel close to Merle and Pearl at the Convent, and that feeling is part of the attraction the place holds for her. The other children are presumably former students of the missionary school, though their identity is never specified. That the house remains filled with these child spirits is the first suggestion of the supernatural in *Paradise*. Morrison's use of such elements is one reason her work is frequently associated with magical realism, though many literary critics and Morrison herself have traced the mystical aspect of her works to black folk culture traditions.

K.D. and the Feud between the Morgans and the Fleetwoods

Of the women at the convent, only Gigi becomes directly involved with people in Ruby. Immediately after she gets off the bus, her suggestive outfit draws K.D.'s attention. He is dating Arnette Fleetwood but takes no responsibility for her pregnancy. We get the account of the fight at the Oven on the day of Gigi's arrival from K.D.'s point-of-view. He remembers the events as he brushes his uncle Steward's dogs Good and Ben, and his gentleness with them softens the harsh picture of his character formed by his actions on that past day.

Arnette and K.D. blame each other for her pregnancy, and even though we get the story from him, his account is unsparing. When he asked her what she planned to do, he was thinking, "You cornered me at more socials than I can remember and when I finally agreed I didn't have to take your drawers down you beat me to it so this ain't my problem" (54). The run-on sentence lends a sense of urgency to his thoughts. When K.D. looks at Gigi, Arnette makes a snide remark, and he slaps her. The townspeople's contempt for overtly sexual women, as shown in chapter 1, supports K.D.'s blaming Arnette for her pregnancy, if not his violence.

The slap from K.D. leads to a meeting between the Morgans and the Fleetwoods, K.D.'s and Arnette's families. The meeting set off one of the main power struggles in the town. Steward and Deek Morgan were leaders in the founding of Ruby, just as their grandfather had been a leader in the founding of Haven. But their power is also economic—they own the town bank, and the Fleetwoods owe the bank money. The twins accompany their nephew to the Fleetwood household. K.D. realizes that he is his uncles' ". . . hope and their despair" (55). Since Deek's sons were killed in Vietnam, K.D. is the only male Morgan heir, despite his disappointing behavior. K.D. realizes his uncles may have an interest in Arnette's pregnancy, because a male child could further the Morgan line. K.D. is nevertheless confident that his uncles will protect him. While Arnette's pregnancy is the subtext of the meeting between the families, it is never mentioned. The conversation focuses solely on K.D.'s hitting Arnette in public.

The meeting is negotiated by Reverend Misner, who, though relatively new to the town, ministers at the Baptist church, which has the largest of Ruby's three congregations. The three Morgan men meet with him before the meeting at the Fleetwoods. Steward and Deek are suspicious of Misner: he has established a non-profit credit union that Steward fears could become competition for the bank. Misner also had a reputation for encouraging political involvement in Civil Rights issues. Such direct conflict with whites is contrary to Steward and Deek's practice of responding to racism by avoiding whites. Readers learn later learn that Steward had publicly opposed a sit-in at a drugstore in Oklahoma City and Thurgood Marshall's represention of the NAACP in an antisegregation lawsuit in Norman, Oklahoma.

The divisions between Misner and Steward represent a historical division in black leadership at the national level. Earlier in the twentieth century, Booker T. Washington was recognized as the most prominent leader of black people, especially by white Americans. Washington believed that black Americans had to temporarily accept their inferior position and that in time they would gain white respect through their hard work and economic gains. W. E. B. DuBois, initially a supporter of Washington's ideas, came to believe that black people needed to demand civil rights and social justice. While the parallel between the literary characters and the historical figures is not exact, both divisions are similarly based on different attitudes toward black activism as a response to white racism. In the book, Misner later thinks to himself that in Ruby, ". . . Booker T. solutions trumped DuBois' problems every time" (212). Ironically, Steward's position aligns him with the leader who received approbation from white people who feared and tried to limit black people's rise in social, political, and economic status.

When the two families meet, Arnette's brother Jeff Fleetwood is the most outspoken and offended of the Fleetwoods, though their father Arnold agrees to the deal they strike. Tragic events in Jeff's life have made him prone to anger. A veteran of the Vietnam War, he has four children who are extremely sick and require constant care. Many literary critics have taken the children's illness as a sign that the town's isolation has led to birth defects caused by inbreeding, though Jeff's exposure to Agent Orange is another possible cause of the birth defects.

K.D. agrees to apologize to Arnette, but that does little to dissipate Jeff's hostility. Deek's suggestion that he and his brother could help with Arnette's college expenses, however, does. Arnold agrees to the deal, with his wife's approval. Steward asks whether Arnette might change plans to attend college in the fall, alluding to Arnette's pregnancy. Arnold's insistence that he will guarantee her enrollment effectively ensures the Morgans that Arnette will get an abortion. Misner remains unaware of Arnette's pregnancy, though he senses the tension at the meeting and realizes that there is something he does not know.

Years later, when K.D. is still involved with Gigi, Deek wonders if he and his brother made the right decision by helping their nephew sever ties with Arnette. To Deek, the Convent is akin to a "brothel . . . where the entrance to hell is wide" (114); Gigi is not one of the eligible women the uncles hoped K.D. would choose. After Gigi leaves K.D., his uncles convince him to marry Arnette.

Grace/Gigi

Gigi is a spirited, sexy woman, always searching for something. She searches for a rock formation that appears to be a couple making love that her boyfriend Mikey told her was in his hometown. They were involved in a Civil Rights protest, and Mikey had been sent to prison. They planned to meet in Wish, Arizona, after his release, but she cannot find a town of that name. Eventually, she gives up her search for him, but not for the rocks. After a stay in Mexico, she calls her grandfather in Alcorn, Mississippi, to tell him she is coming home. To mark the civil unrest of the time, Morrison has the grandfather recite a list of assassinations of Civil Rights leaders that have occurred since she left: Medgar Evers in 1963; Malcolm X in 1965; Martin Luther King, Jr. and Robert Kennedy in 1968. This conversation indicates that Gigi has been away from home for at least five years.

On her way home, she meets a man on a train who tells her about two trees that grow together in Ruby. The legend is "if you squeezed in between them in just the right way, . . . you would feel an ecstasy no human could invent or duplicate" (66). So Gigi heads instead for Ruby. Disappointed by the small country town with no hotel and boys who remind her of Alcorn, Mississippi, she immediately decides to leave. She gets a ride from Roger Best, the town's mortician, who is headed to the Convent to pick up the body of Mother, who has died. Gigi remains at the Convent when Connie asks her to stay while she sleeps.

While Ruby's men oppose the sinfulness of wanton sexuality, for the women at the Convent, sex implies menace. Their experiences, though extreme, reflect the pervasive danger sex poses to women in a male-dominated society. Even Gigi, the woman most comfortable with her own sexuality, recognizes the potential threat as she notices the sexually suggestive statues, doorknobs, and plumbing fixtures throughout the house. She thinks of the pleasure men would take flicking their cigars into vagina-shaped ashtrays and is disturbed by the picture of a kneeling Saint Catherine of Siena offering her breasts on a platter. The woman's "I give up" face haunts Gigi and takes the pleasure out of the power her own body wields over K.D. when he comes to take her for a drive later that day (74). Her agitation does not take away her own pleasure in her body, however, and Mavis returns to the Convent to find a naked Gigi sunbathing.

In the three years since her arrival at the Convent, Mavis has developed a protective, exclusive bond with Connie and her new home and resents Gigi's intrusion. Mavis's reaction to Gigi shows that the impulse to exclude others is not unique to the citizens of Ruby. But Connie, whose alcoholism makes her a dubious leader, assures Mavis that she will come to like Gigi. Nevertheless, the two women's fights escalate that day until they are interrupted by Arnette, who arrives seeking help, claiming she has been raped.

Gigi carries on an affair with K.D., taking advantage of his obsessive passion and resulting devotion. But when he becomes angry at her capriciousness and hits her, she ends the relationship. She convinces herself that she is staying at the Convent only to unearth the treasure in the box she found in the floor beneath the tub. But she never leaves because she cannot decide where to go or what to do. When she first left home to become active in the Civil Rights Movement, she was serious about her commitment. She is disappointed in herself for becoming distracted by fun and for her failure to maintain steadfast commitment to the cause.

Dovey and Steward Morgan, and the Fight Over the Oven

Steward's wife, Dovey, provides much of the insight into his character. Her concern about her husband and community also explains many of the ideas and events dividing the townspeople. Dovey recognizes that Steward's ambition undercuts his success as well as his satisfaction. In Dovey's view, each of Steward's recent achievements has been met with a corresponding loss. "Almost always, these nights, when Dovey Morgan thought about her husband, it was in terms of what he had lost. . . . Contrary to his (and all of Ruby's) assessment, the more Steward acquired, the more visible his losses" (82). His gains have been financial, his losses personal and spiritual. His enjoyment of food, for example, has been undermined by his chewing tobacco habit and also by his unrealistic expectations, which developed from his dreams of home cooking when he was a soldier. Steward's exalted expectations likewise leave him dissatisfied with the town he helped create. Just as his sense of taste has grown so dull that he craves only the Convent's hot pepper (making his nourishment ironically dependent upon the women he abhors), his ability to sense the town's needs likewise has diminished. Steward's reaction to food distinguishes him from his brother Deek, who relished his first meals after the war. This difference foreshadows the disparity between the brothers at the end of the novel, as they must reconcile themselves to their part in the raid on the Convent and the townspeople's reaction to it. Deek is the brother who is able to change; Steward becomes more resolute in his own position.

Dovey's musings also convey the generational tensions in Ruby. The younger generation's discontent is represented by individual erratic behavior as well as by arguments with older town members over the meaning and exact wording of the Oven's worn inscription. Dovey's thoughts reveal their actions, which are taken by the men to be signs of the Convent's evil influence. Details that help explain the actions are revealed later in the novel. Arnette, no doubt suffering from depression brought on by the loss of her baby, spends her college vacation in bed. Menus is developing a drinking problem, ostensibly in reaction to his experiences in Vietnam, though we later learn that his continual drunkenness may also result from regret for letting members of the town convince him not to marry the light-skinned woman he loves. Billie Delia has left town and no one knows where she has gone. Sweetie Fleetwood, Jeff's wife, laughs all the time; the demands of constantly caring for her ill children are leading to a nervous breakdown. And K.D. is having a scandalous affair with Gigi. Dovey has discussed these problems with other women in the town, though they reach no consensus.

The argument over the Oven, which began with the young people of the Baptist congregation, Misner's church, and soon spread to members of the Methodist and Pentecostal congregations, is the main manifestation of discontent in the town. Just as he had to settle the problem between the Morgans and Fleetwoods, Misner once again arranges a meeting to discuss the matter, this time inviting the whole town. The young people's forcefulness disturbs their parents, who are also offended by references to Haven's founders as "ex-slaves" (84). The young people believe the original inscription on the Oven read "Be the Furrow of His Brow," which they interpret as a call to activism but which the older members of the community find irreverent. The elders believe that the original inscription read "Beware the

Furrow of His Brow," a caution to remain properly respectful and de-
vout, but the youth find this interpretation inappropriately sub-
servient. Ultimately, the meeting disintegrates into a fight not only
between young and old, but between Reverends Misner and Pulliam,
the leaders who side with them. Steward, who believes that the young
people are really saying "Cut me some slack" (93), ends the meeting
by threatening to kill anyone who changes the Oven's inscription. His
threat increases Dovey's concern about him.

After the meeting that night, Dovey chooses to stay at the small
house they own in town, while Steward goes to their farm, which he
prefers. They cannot agree on which residence will be their perma-
nent home. One of the reasons Dovey prefers the house on St.
Matthews Street is because she receives visits from her mysterious
Friend there. The Friend may be a man or may be a spiritual presence. He first appeared in her backyard one day following a burst of
butterflies. Her attraction to him is based on how attentively he listens to her, no matter how trivial her topic, giving her the leisure to
discuss whatever she may wish. By contrast, Steward clearly has min-
imal listening skills, though he loves his wife deeply.

Soane

Soane Morgan is Deacon's wife and both Dovey's sister and sister-
in-law. Thoughtful like Dovey, she worries about her husband and
town. Her interior monologues provide details that help explain
many of the ongoing stories in the novel. Soane spends her days making lace, and her nephew K.D. wonders about his aunt's work habits:
"Aunt Soane worked thread like a prisoner: daily, methodically, for
free, producing more lace than could ever be practical" (53). Her
excessive work is one indication of her troubled mind and also shows
the absence of meaningful work for her. Soane and her sister were

both schoolteachers before they married, and Soane continued to teach for a while. But the town does not provide many work opportunities for the women; they are expected to be wives. Such expectations represent the norm of middle class life in the United States at the time, though those traditional roles were beginning to be challenged. While the rising political activism of Ruby's youth focuses on racial and not gender issues, Arnette and Billie Delia's problems reveal that the limited expectations and opportunities for women are also a source of Ruby's trouble.

Soane is first introduced in the second chapter when she visits the Convent shortly after Mavis's arrival there. She has come to get Connie's help. Soane is reintroduced later in the novel, after a second trip to get help from Connie, with whom she has become a close friend. The mysterious bundle Connie gives Soane contains an abortifacient, and Soane regrets the first time she sought such help, remembering that her daughter would now be nineteen. As she prepares the medicine, she also thinks of her sons, Scout and Easter, who were killed in Vietnam. After they enlisted, Menus Jury and Jeff Fleetwood had returned alive from their tours of duty. Given the increasing racial violence in the country, Soane believed that her sons would actually be safer as soldiers than as black men in the United States anywhere outside of Ruby.

Like her sister Dovey, Soane has communication problems with her husband. She has not told Deek of her pregnancy. While Steward surveys his farm and goes horseback riding to clear his head after the town meeting, Deek goes hunting. Soane's irritation with her spouse is revealed in her attitude to his sport: "Look out, quail. Deek's gunning for you. And when he comes back he'll throw a sackful of you on my clean floor and say something like: 'This ought to take care of supper.' Proud. Like he's giving me a present. Like you were already plucked, cleaned, and cooked" (100). Whereas Dovey sees Steward's ambition as his fault, Soane sees pride as Deek's. For instance, he takes immense joy in driving his expensive black car to the bank every day, even though the trip is less than a mile.

Dovey and Soane's ruminations lead them both from concerns about their husbands to problems in Ruby. But the sisters' private lives are similar in other ways as well. Just as Dovey has a mysterious visitor, Soane, after her miscarriage, saw a woman in antiquated dress carrying an empty basket. Soane interpreted her vision as a symbol of the remorse and loneliness she would suffer. Dovey's visitor, by contrast, seems to assuage her loneliness.

That the women's emotional estrangement from their husbands relates to the men's misogyny is clearer perhaps in Soane's interactions with Deek than in Dovey's with Steward. Soane's irritated response to her husband's hunting and trivial habits, such as his not putting his coat and boots in the closet as he undresses, covers more meaningful differences. She is incensed by his saying that Gigi "dragged" herself into town and corrects him, which suggests that she is angry about his attitude toward women. That he condescendingly says that she does not need to understand shifts in the town's economy as long as he does shows that he is demeaning to her as well as to the Convent women, albeit to a much lesser degree.

Soane is confused, not by the economical principles of credit and debt, but by the change in her husband: ". . . she didn't understand why he wasn't worried enough by their friends' money problems to help them out" (107). Deek likewise remembers that Haven survived the Depression of the 1930s because neighbors helped one another, sharing profits from the crops that prospered with those whose crops failed. With fondness and pride, he recollects the former townspeople's loyalty: "Having been refused by the world in 1890 on their journey to Oklahoma, Haven residents refused each other nothing, were vigilant to any need or shortage" (109). But he does not recognize the change in his own behavior as he discusses his current neighbors' misfortunes.

Like Dovey's reflections, Soane's give us another perspective on the generational conflict in Ruby. Soane worries about the troubled young people who spend time at the Oven. Someone painted a black fist with red nails on the Oven, and Soane finds it a portentous sign. While her response to the young people's outrage is more sympathetic than Deek's or Steward's, she cannot relate to it. Like her husband and brother-in-law, she feels protected from racism in Ruby and desires no interaction with the outside world. Even though Dovey and Soane recognize their husbands' limitations and the changes in their community, they, like their husbands, believe that any significant threat to their peaceful existence is external. They cannot understand why the young people act as if the problem is internal. Thus, Dovey cannot identify the source of their anger because "there were no whites (moral or malevolent) around to agitate or incense them" (102). Yet she resents their acting as if their perceptions about white people are new or unique, and she finds the connection the young people feel to Africa even more inexplicable.

Soane hears in the young people's speech an "accusation" against all the founders of Ruby (and by implication, Haven) for the choice to move away from white people in order to evade their racism. The young people seek direct confrontation and act "as though there was a new and more manly way to deal with whites . . . some African-type thing full of new words, new color combinations and new haircuts. Suggesting that outsmarting whites was craven. That they had to be told, rejected, confronted. Because the old way was slow, limited to just a few, and weak" (104). In many if not most ways, the generational conflict in Ruby is typical of the generational conflict experienced throughout the United States in response to the Civil Rights and Black Power movements of the 1960s. By the late 1960s and 1970s, such conflict had become widespread as younger generations' demands became more forceful. Protests to the Vietnam War also fueled the generational divisiveness. The novel shows that Ruby's isolation cannot give them immunity to the changes in the country; separatism does not provide protection.

Anna Flood, Patricia Best, and Richard Misner: The Love Triangle

Dovey and Soane are not the only characters who show that Ruby's women hold different visions of their town than do the men. Anna Flood, who had moved to Detroit, returned after her father Ace's death. When Misner came to town, she decided to stay and run Ace's Grocery, rejuvenating the business in the process. Less provincial than those who have never left Ruby, Anna's openness to change is shown by more than her ability to adapt the store to changing times. She wears her hair natural, and people's reaction to it tells her much about them. (She suspects that some women were jealous of her relationship with Misner not just because of their own hopes upon the eligible bachelor's arrival, but also because he chose someone who does not straighten her hair.) She also tells Misner that she went to Detroit because she wanted to " . . . do something up north. Something real that wouldn't break my heart" (118). Their mutual interest in social change is no doubt one reason for their courtship. Adaptable and perceptive, Anna nevertheless clings to her expectation for Ruby to possess a community spirit. Where Misner sees capitalism, she knows the town's history and remembers that first Haven and then Ruby developed from the people's cooperation. She refutes Misner's description of Ruby as Steward and Morgan's town. And when he explains that he meant they control things because they have money and run the bank, Anna explains that everyone contributed to the founding of the banks, first in Haven and then in Ruby. Misner sees the Morgans' profit motive;

Anna expects them to be true to the town's historical values. Their more open disagreement recalls Soane and Deek's earlier discussion of town economics and Soane's wondering why her husband did not help their neighbors.

When Steward comes into the store, Richard and Anna are helping a lost white couple with an ill baby. The woman will not enter the store, no doubt because she is in an all-black town. Steward's reaction reveals the extent of his animosity toward white people and further distinguishes his attitude from Misner's. Steward describes white people as " . . . born lost. Take over the world and still lost." But when he seeks agreement from Richard, Misner reminds him that "God has one people." Undaunted, Steward rejects this guidance from his minister, declaring, "Richard . . . I've heard you say things *out* of ignorance, but this is the first time I heard you say something *based* on ignorance" (123). Steward's suspicion of outsiders and contempt for whites predominate his thoughts and overshadow all other lessons he learned from the history of the town he knows so well. That the lost couple fail to heed the warnings about the oncoming blizzard suggests that their own sense of racial superiority undermines their judgment, as their dead bodies are discovered later.

Seneca

As they talk in the store, Steward mentions to Richard and Anna that earlier that morning Deek saw Sweetie Fleetwood walking down the street in her nightgown, and Richard adds that he also saw her. Sweetie has not left her home in six years because she has, with help from her mother-in-law, maintained vigilant watch over her sick children all that time. (Her husband and father-in-law cannot bear the children's illness, so their care falls to the women of the household.) But that morning after her night watch, she fears that if she goes to bed, she will never be able to get up and care for her children again. The endless repetition of her routine becomes too much for her: "The small thing she wanted was not to have that dawn coffee, the already drawn bath, the folded nightgown and then the watchful sleep in that order, forever, every day and in particular this here particular day. The only way to change the order, she thought, was not to do something differently, but to do a different thing" (125). Described immediately after Steward's display of the rigidity of his position—and he is the character in the novel most opposed to change—Sweetie's dazed yet purposeful walk though the town shows that stasis is unhealthy for any thing, person or town.

Sweetie's walk also sets the mood for Seneca's entrance; the sorrow of the first woman draws the second from her hiding place in the back of a truck passing through town. Abandoned when she was five, Seneca spent two days knocking on every door in the apartment building looking for her sister. On the third day, she decides that if she behaves well enough, Jean (who turns out to be her mother, not her sister) will return. As she looks out the window for her sister, she sees a woman crying on the street, and the image of that woman will continue to haunt Seneca, who herself never cries. On the fifth day Seneca finds a note written in lipstick, which she cannot read, in a box of Lorna Doone cookies. She carries that note with her for the rest of her life.

Sweetie allows Seneca to place a wrap around her shoulders and walk with her, though she thinks of the stranger as Sin incarnate, as if she were in a morality play. She herself feels that she is in a state of grace and is warmed by the layer of snow that covers her. When they reach the Convent, the women there seem like hawks to her, and she refuses their offers of food and drink. Like Mavis, Sweetie hears children in the house. She is awakened by the sound of a baby's cry, which enthralls her because her own children are mute. But the sound infuriates her as she realizes that ". . . babies cry here among these demons but not in her house" (130). She demands to leave and meets her husband, Jeff, and Anna Flood, who have come to look for her. Sweetie claims that the Convent women " . . . made me, snatched me" (130), and her accusations add to the rumors and suspicions about the Convent. Unlike on the previous day's journey, during her return home she is fearful for her children and very cold.

Seneca, on the other hand, is welcomed by Gigi and Mavis and immediately recognizes the women's mutual animosity. She placates them both; abandonment had made her ever-agreeable, lest she be unloved again. Her vulnerability has made her an easy target for people who want to use her. She has recently been involved with a man who was imprisoned for running over a child with his car. After a six-month relationship that provides relative security to Seneca, Eddie Turtle learns that he can treat her badly. He demands that she bring him shoes and a bible and responds angrily because he does not like the bible she chose. When she visits him in prison, he asks about his dogs, not about her. She notices how tender the other inmates are with their visiting families and foolishly hopes that Eddie will become caring like them in the future. Nevertheless, she leaves promising to fulfill more of his commands.

One of Eddie's orders was for Seneca to convince his mother to cash a savings bond and bring him the money. Mrs. Turtle, however, is not as naïve as Seneca and refused to help the son she knows is guilty. But after Seneca leaves her home, she sees Eddie's mother sobbing. The crying woman evokes Seneca's own grief, and she runs to the bus station. There, she is approached by yet another person who wants to use her.

A chauffeur offers Seneca " . . . five hundred dollars for some complicated but quite easy work" (135) and introduces her to the elegant Mrs. Norma Keene Fox, who is waiting in a limousine.

Norma implies that she needs an assistant for some kind of secretarial work, but she really seeks a sex worker. Though free to leave, Seneca submits, as she is accustomed to do; her defining characteristic is her willingness to please others. While she was " . . . well cared for, loved, perhaps, by the mothers in both of the foster homes, she knew it was not her self that the mothers had approved of but the fact that she took reprimand quietly, ate what given, shared what she had and never ever cried" (135). Norma's impersonal detachment (she does not even ask Seneca's name) therefore seems familiar to her. When Norma's husband calls to announce his arrival, Seneca is summarily dismissed, paid, and returned to the bus station. Not knowing what to do, she travels by hiding in trucks as a secret passenger, until she sees Sweetie and ends up at the Convent. Following Sweetie represents a change for Seneca—it ". . . was the first pointedly uninstructed thing she had ever done" (138). However small and random an act, Seneca had made a choice about her life.

Seneca cuts her skin to manifest and control pain. Her first cut was accidental and happened when a boy in her foster home raped her. She received sympathy for the cut but was sent away for telling that she was raped. Because she is repeatedly sexually assaulted by men, she assumes that she attracts the abuse and that it is her fault. When the peace she finds at the Convent is disturbed by Pallas's constant crying, a sound Seneca cannot bear, she turns again to the comfort of cutting herself.

K.D. and Arnette's Wedding

Presided over by the two ministers, Reverends Pulliam and Misner, K.D. and Arnette's wedding is less a celebration of a union than the drawing of battle lines. The men's sermons intensify the tensions among the townspeople, who had been hoping that the marriage would end the antagonisms between the Morgans and the Fleetwoods. Pulliam, the Methodist minister, delivers a fire-and-brimstone sermon that emphasizes the difficulty of love and human unworthiness of it. Anna Flood considers that Pulliam may have been admonishing the young people, but decides that his words are aimed at Misner, the newer preacher with the larger congregation who has helped organize the young people and encouraged their dissent.

Misner also interprets Pulliam's sermon as a personal attack and is angry at Pulliam's usurpation of the wedding ceremony to escalate their philosophical, political, and personal battles. In response, Misner decides not to speak; instead, he removes the cross from the back wall and holds it up as a symbol to the congregation. He intends for the cross to be both a unifying symbol and a reminder of Christ, whose existence is proof that " . . . God loved the way humans loved one another; loved the way humans loved themselves" (146). But Misner's message fails to reach the people, who sit confused in the awkward silence.

K D., feeling the pressure of his family's and the townspeople's expectations, is angry that his marriage is being used for so many other purposes. He is ready to end the rumors about him, appease his uncles, and join " . . . the married and propertied men of Ruby" (147). But mostly he seeks vindication against Gigi, who has turned him away although his passion for her remains strong. His thoughts about her are virulent; he wants " . . . to flush that Gigi bitch out of his life completely. Like sugar turning from unreasonable delight to the body's mortal enemy, his craving for her had poisoned him, rendered him diabetic, stupid, helpless. . . . Most of all he had loved her for years, an aching, humiliating, self-loathing love that drifted from pining to stealth" (147). Finally, K.D. wants to burn the dozen letters Arnette sent him from college. He read only the first, refusing to believe that Arnette understands passion the way he does. His feelings toward her suggest that his marriage does not mirror those of the previous Moran generation. Rather, it magnifies their male condescension while retaining none of the love. Marriage is yet another disintegrating social practice.

Arnette, on the other hand, is horrified by Misner's actions. Lacking a sense of self, her identity has been based solely on her love for K.D.: "She believed she loved him absolutely because he was all she knew about her self—which was to say, everything she knew of her body was connected to him. Except for Billie Delia, no one had told her there was any other way to think of herself" (148). K.D.'s proposal had made her happy and had seemed to cure her pain, returning her sense of identity and purpose. But as she anxiously waits for Misner to begin reading the wedding vows, her feelings of loss return, and she realizes that her emptiness is based not only on the loss of K.D., but also on the loss of their child several years earlier. Later that night, she goes to the Convent and demands her baby. She is disoriented, just as her sister-in-law, Sweetie, had been on her visit to the Convent. Arnette had sought refuge at the Convent during her pregnancy and had delivered a baby, but it survived only a few days, damaged by Arnette's repeated attempts to induce a miscarriage. Arnette physically attacks the women at the Convent when they cannot produce her child, and she accuses them of stealing it.

Watching Misner, Steward thinks of all the times he has seen the cross misused and appropriated for evil purposes, such as being burned in the yards of black families to intimidate them. The violence and evil Steward has seen in his life have so traumatized him that he sees them everywhere. Soane, meanwhile, worries about the mood shift from peaceful to anxious. Believing that the day would be a happy celebration, she has invited the women at the Convent to the wedding reception she is hosting. But due to the tone of the wedding ceremony, she fears the women will not be welcomed by her other guests and there might be trouble. Connie does not attend the party, but the other four women—Mavis, Gigi, Seneca, and Pallas—do. They are dressed inappropriately, " . . . looking like go-go girls" (156), and they join some of the young people who have wandered to the Oven, where they dance to music loud enough to reach Soane's house and disturb the reception. They even borrow and ride children's bikes. But while their antics disturb many of the guests, they also provide a distraction that dissipates the tensions aroused by the wedding ceremony.

Billie Delia

Billie Delia is Pat Best's daughter and Arnette's best friend. She was branded with a bad reputation at an early age. Treated as an outcast and viewed with suspicion, she has developed a critical outsider's perspective of Ruby through which she watches Arnette's wedding. She sees the futility of the attempt to heal the conflict between the families through the marriage. Beyond rumors about what happened to Arnette while she was at the Convent, Billie Delia senses a power struggle between the men and their desire to control women. She thinks that " . . . the real battle was not about infant life or a bride's reputation but about disobedience, which meant, of course, the stallions were fighting about who controlled the mares and their foals" (150). Billie Delia's use of equine imagery is fitting because her first sexual experience and public shame were related to horses.

As a child, Billie Delia loved to ride Nathan DuPres's horse whenever he came to town. Unaccustomed to regularly wearing underpants, one Sunday, in front of everyone, preparing to mount the horse, she removed the pair she was wearing that day. She was too young to understand the sexual implications of her act and was therefore confused by everyone's reactions. Her mother meted out an incomprehensible punishment and became watchful of her daughter's behavior. Nathan offers her no more horse rides, her peers tease her, boys view her sexually, and adults become uncomfortable around her because she reminds them of their own sexuality, which they have tried to suppress. Soane and Dovey Morgan and Anna Flood were kind and did not judge her. These three women are also among the minority in Ruby who are tolerant, if not accepting, of the women at the Convent.

Despite her reputation, Billie Delia is in fact a virgin. She is hopelessly in love with two brothers, Apollo and Brood Poole, and cannot choose between them. When her mother finds her with the two brothers, they have a physical fight that leaves Billie Delia with a split lip and a black eye. She runs first to Anna Flood and then to the Convent. Her stay there is a transforming experience: " . . . what she saw and learned there changed her forever" (152), and when she leaves she moves to Demby and gets a job in a medical clinic.

Pallas Truelove

At the clinic, Billie Delia meets the traumatized Pallas Truelove, whom she takes to the Convent. Pallas is in shock and does not speak for her first three days there. Chased by men who may have raped her, she escaped capture by hiding in a lake at night, and she still actively fears the dark water. She encountered the men after running away from her mother's home and getting lost. Pallas was raised by her father, a wealthy lawyer, and enjoyed a privileged upbringing. Her mother had left the family when Pallas was three, and at sixteen Pallas decides to visit her mother on Christmas. She takes along her boyfriend of four months, Carlos, an artist who works as her school's maintenance man. Pallas's mother, Divine, or Dee Dee, Truelove, is also an artist, and Pallas and Carlos stay with her in New Mexico for several happy months. But when Pallas discovers her mother and Carlos making love, she drives away and gets lost, the event that leads to the incident at the lake. She is picked up by an Indian family that takes her to the clinic where she meets Billie Delia.

Once Pallas meets Connie, she feels safe at the Convent: " . . . the whole house felt permeated with a blessed malelessness, like a protected domain, free of hunters but exciting too. As though she might meet herself here—an unbridled, authentic self" (177). The Convent provides for these women who are haunted by the violence in their past, a place free from judgment where they can recover, or recreate, themselves. When they return from the wedding reception, they dance together in the kitchen, " . . . first, apart, imagining partners. Then partnered, imagining each other" (179). Despite their bickering, the gift they give each other is the space to reimagine themselves and their lives.

Pallas eventually returns to her own home, which she finds insufferable. Rumors have made her an outcast and a joke at school, and her angry father pursues a futile lawsuit against the school, insisting that their employee, Carlos, had harmed his daughter. She convinces him to let her visit his sister in Chicago and then leaves her aunt's to return to the Convent. She is pregnant, though she denies it when Connie tells her so.

Pat Best

Billie Delia's mother, Pat Best, is the town schoolteacher. She has been working on an annotated genealogy of Ruby's fifteen founding families, a task made more difficult by the townspeople's reticence. Their secrecy annoys her and fosters suspicions as her research reveals many inconsistencies in the town's stories. To Pat, the most significant feature of the original founding families and their descendents is the racial purity signified by their dark black skin, a quality she calls eight-rock, for a low level in coal mines. Pat suspects that this characteristic makes them feel superior, a feeling resulting from the discrimination they suffered during Reconstruction as they learned that light skin was prized even among African-Americans:

For ten generations they had believed the division they fought to close was free against slave and rich against poor. Usually, but not always, white against black. Now they saw a new separation: light-skinned against black. Oh, they knew there was a difference in the minds of whites, but it had not struck them before that it was of consequence, serious consequence, to Negroes themselves. (194)

Based on this theory, Pat believes the words on the Oven read "Beware the Furrow of His Brow," which she interprets as a reference to the Disallowing, a warning to the light-skinned people of Fairly who turned the Haven settlers away. This concept of racial purity is based on physical features and the line of descent from ancestors in the Louisiana Territory. While Pat believes there is a miscegenation taboo in the town, her descriptions of the very straight hair of the Blackhorse family, as well as the surname itself, indicate an unacknowledged Native American ancestry.

World War II disrupted Haven's separatism when grandsons of the town founders became soldiers. Pat feels that the disrespect shown to those men in their own country when they returned from war intensified their commitment to separatism and to protecting their eight-rock purity. Many of them disapproved of her father Roger Best's marriage to a woman with skin light enough that she could pass for white, none louder than Steward, who said, "He's bringing along the dung we leaving behind." In response, Fairy DuPres put a curse on Steward: "God don't love ugly ways. Watch out He don't deny you what you love" (201). Pat believes that her parents' marriage is the source of her father's unpopularity, not, as he believes, that he prepared his wife Delia's body for burial. Delia died in childbirth while Roger was away at mortuary school and some members of the town were offended that he was the mortician of his own wife. Many Ruby women, including Dovey Morgan, begged the men to go to the Convent to get one of the nuns who might be able to help the ailing Delia, but the men would not and the women could not drive. Although her father does not agree, Pat suspects that the men would not go for help because they did not want to seek it from white people and because they resented Delia's light skin.

Pat, who felt shunned as a child because of her light skin, married Billy Cato partially for the darkness of his, but their daughter Billie Delia inherits her mother's lighter skin. And Billy dies so soon after marriage that everyone still referred to Pat by her maiden name, which may be another sign that she is being shut out from the eight-rock families. As she works on her notes, Pat reconsiders her relationship with her daughter and how it has been affected by the town's racial prejudices. Having seen Billie Delia entangled with the Poole brothers behind the Oven, Pat believes her daughter is having a sexual affair with the brothers, though Billie Delia insists she is not. Pat tries to understand how she could have become violent in their resulting fight and realizes that she has always been judgmental of her daughter. She suspects that if Billie Delia were not light-skinned, her reputation would not have been permanently ruined when she removed her panties to ride the horse when she was only three years old. And Pat wonders if she herself has internalized the bias toward dark skin as well as the town's condemnation of her daughter: " . . . the question for her now in the silence of this here night was whether she had defended Billie Delia or sacrificed her" (203).

Pat's focus on exclusion carries over to the Christmas pageant, where she talks with Richard Misner. Each year the children put on a play that combines the story of Joseph and Mary's being turned away from the inns in Bethlehem with that of the Disallowing, though the children's play represents only seven of the nine founding families. Two have been dropped for reasons Misner does not understand and Pat cannot figure out. Pat and Richard have a disagreement about teaching. Pat wonders if the activism Richard encourages is not too militant; he thinks the history she teaches is too complacent. He tries to convince her that recognizing their African heritage is important, but she says she feels no connection to Africa. Because of her theories about eight-rock heritage and exclusion, Pat sees dangers in Misner's attraction to Africa as a homeland. He had hoped she would become an ally and not be threatened by the changes he and the young people he taught were encouraging. She defends the traditional position of the town with a passion she does not feel. He continues to feel excluded from the town and tells her that he is " . . . an outsider . . . not an enemy." She reminds him that in Ruby those are the same (212). She later regrets her behavior toward him, mimicking as it does the attitude she has herself resented. When she goes home, she burns all her notes about the town and almost immediately regrets doing so.

Connie

Connie has lived with Mother in the Convent since she was nine and knows no other life. Mother, then called Sister Mary Magna because she had not yet become mother superior and gained her nickname, rescued the orphaned, homeless child. After Mother's death, she feels lost, so she drinks the wine in the cellar and waits to die. Though the women at the Convent feel loved by her, she has grown weary of their stories and, with the exception of Mavis, can barely distinguish one from another. She is annoyed by their lingering and dreaminess and angry at their constant tales of romantic love because her own experience has left her bitter.

Connie worked at the Convent, devoted to Mother and to Christ for 30 years. Raped as a child, she had no interest in men all those years. But on a trip to Ruby, Connie meets Deacon and falls in love. Disturbed by her feelings, she stays at the Convent to avoid him. But he comes there to buy peppers, and they begin an affair. Connie has her own dreams of love and domesticity, which she based around the burned-down farmhouse in the field where she and Deek spent their Friday afternoons. Deek stops his visits when Connie's passion seems too intense, and one day Soane, not realizing that her husband has ended the affair, arrives at the Convent, seeking Connie's help. Her presence makes Deek's marriage a reality to Connie, who realizes now that he will not visit again. Soane believes that Deek will end the affair if he knows that she is willing to end her pregnancy because of it. Connie does not give her an abortifacient, but Soane loses the baby anyway. She believes her miscarriage is punishment for her threat.

After the affair ends, Connie renews her faith. Lone DuPres begins to visit and talk of magic, but Connie rejects Lone's suggestions because of her faith. But when Soane's drunk fifteen-year-old son Scout crashes the truck he is driving, Connie becomes willing to try Lone's practice. Lone, who is visiting Connie, senses the danger and takes her to the scene of the crash. Following Lone's directions, Connie enters the dead boy's body and leads him back to life. Connie is horrified by what she has done because she believes her actions are sinful, but Lone insists that the power is a gift from God. Lone tells Soane that Connie has saved her son, and Soane goes to Connie to thank her, beginning their friendship. Connie again uses her ability to keep Mary Magna alive, although she knows the woman would abhor the practice.

Connie's gifts develop, making her aware of what is happening with others. As her gifts intensify, she receives a mystical visit from a man whose physical features—long tea-colored hair and large, round, apple-green eyes—recall her own when Mary Magna found her, making him seem a male version of herself. When she was obsessed with Deek, she felt that being with him was being home. In fact, part of her initial attraction to him lay in the familiarity of the celebration of the dark-skinned people she saw in town, which reminded her of home. With the visitation, her original home returns to her. The danger of this narrative move, following the novel's logic, is that with it Morrison posits an original, true home that provides a healing religion, one that precedes the soul–body dualism of Christianity. As we have seen in the myth of Haven and Pat's suspicion of Misner's embracing Africa as the true home, such perfect origins have been posited as illusory and dangerous. The question then becomes whether such myths are indeed destructive or whether Haven was conceived with a faulty philosophy.

Connie transforms and takes charge of the women at the Convent. She prepares a feast and informs them that she is Consolata Sosa and they must obey her. She instructs them to clean the cellar floor and lie on it. She paints outlines around their bodies and gives a sermon in ungrammatical syntax, as if the grammar of her first language, which she lost, had returned to her. In brief outline she tells her autobiography—how twice a woman saved her soul from her body, referring to Mary Magna's rescue of her as a child and leading her back to her faith after her affair with Deek. But Consolata's message differs from Mother's—her purpose is to return the women to their bodies. She instructs them never to let their soul be separated from their bodies again, asserting that " . . . Eve is Mary's mother. Mary is the daughter of Eve" (263). Consolata thus insists on the union of the two parts into which woman has been divided in Western culture: the sinning flesh and the immaculate soul.

From their positions on the floor, the women begin to tell their stories, which merge into one dream-like monologue. They repeat the story-telling ceremony and help each other piece together the details of their individual stories, working together toward a coherent narrative. At Pallas's suggestion, they also begin to paint the body

outlines on the floor with physical details as well as parts of their stories. Pallas acknowledges her pregnancy by painting a fetus in the
womb of her figure. When Seneca feels compelled to cut herself,
she draws a scar on her representation instead. The stories and the
artwork help the women heal more actively than the Convent had
done up to that point. Before, they were safe, passively seeking comfort and refuge. Now, they actively take control of their stories. When
Soane visits, she notices the crucial difference: " . . . unlike some
people in Ruby, the Convent women were no longer haunted" (266).
Consolata's union of the physical and spiritual worlds may be seen
as a corrective to Ruby's emphasis on spiritual goals and its deni-
gration of the physical, particularly sexuality.

Lone DuPres

Like Connie, Lone was rescued as a child. Fairy DuPres raised her
and taught her to midwife and to heal. Lone has the gift of being able
to know other people's thoughts as well. Her services as midwife are
no longer in demand because Ruby women are choosing to deliver
their babies in the Demby hospital, where they could get a week's rest,
drugs, and care for their newborn infants. Lone suspects that her reputation has been ruined after delivering the deformed Fleetwood babies. Resentful that she has been turned away, Lone ignored the signs
that should have alerted her to danger. After she found the car of the
dead family lost in the blizzard, for instance, she noticed that the men
she showed the car to stared at the Convent in the distance not at it.
So Lone pays attention when she overhears men at the Oven cata-
loguing grievances against the Convent women, culminating with the
accusation that " . . . they don't need men and they don't need God"
(276). The men considered the Convent women an affront to their
image of what a lady should be. Lone attempts to warn the women of

the impending attack but is unsuccessful because Connie is asleep and the others will not wake her or take Lone's warning seriously.

Lone seeks Richard Misner's help, but he and Anna are out of town. She turns to Frances Poole and Sut DuPres, who agrees to alert Reverends Pulliam and Cary the following morning. Unable to find help in town, Lone drives to the outlying farms, but her car breaks down along the way. Finally, she reaches Pious DuPres, who organizes the gathering of a party to stop the attack. They will be too late. Meanwhile, the women at the Convent dance in the rain, finally letting go of the images that have haunted them. Before retiring to bed, they listen to Consolata's story about Piedade, a woman who sings but does not speak. The next morning, three of the women are preparing breakfast when they hear the men and flee, first to the game room and then, after a struggle with some of the men, out of the Convent. A fourth woman enters the kitchen and is shot. Connie is trying to save her when she hears more shots and goes to the next room. She finds Deek, who tries but fails to stop his brother Steward from shooting her just as Soane and Dovey enter.

More people arrive from Ruby, and they seek an explanation. K.D. claims that the women were shot in self-defense. Steward claims that "the evil is in this house." His brother disagrees, breaking what has always been their united front. Deek proclaims, "My brother is lying. This is our doing. Ours alone. And we bear the responsibility" (291). The attack also harms Dovey and Soane's relationship when Soane points out that Steward is the one who shot Connie. The citizens of Ruby realize that the purpose of their town had been destroyed, and they wonder, "How could so clean and blessed a mission devour itself and become the world they had escaped?" (292). Lone stays with the bodies, awaiting the arrival of Roger Best, but when the mortician gets to the Convent, he cannot find any bodies. When Misner returns to town, he is told two stories about what happened, neither of which he believes. The first is that nine men went to the Convent to persuade the women to leave, fought with them, and saw the women disappear. The second version is that five of the men wanted to force the women to leave, while the other four tried to stop them; the women attacked the men and fled, but not before Connie was shot. Hostilities among families in the town are only heightened by what has happened. Deek is the only one of the nine men who has not put forth a self-serving version of events. Deek has been changed by what he has done and confronts his own shame. He begins talking with Richard Misner, trying to explain " . . . his long remorse . . . at having become what the Old Fathers cursed: the kind of man who set himself up to judge, rout, and even destroy the needy, the defenseless, the different" (302).

Save-Marie: A Mystical Ending

Morrison has said that she wanted to begin and end the novel with the violent attack on the Convent, thus, the final chapter functions as a postscript to the action. The chapter begins with the funeral for Save-Marie, one of Sweetie and Jeff's children. As Misner presides, he decides that he will stay in Ruby, suddenly assured of his purpose in this broken town. He and Anna had gone to the Convent to see it for themselves, and they cannot logically explain what happened to the women. While there, they have a vision: she sees a closed door, he sees an open window. Both wonder, but dare not ask, what would happen if they went through the openings and what awaits on the other side.

But the truly mystical element is the continuation of the Convent women's stories. All are reconciled with their family members. Gigi visits her father, a member of a prison work crew. Pallas's mother, Dee Dee, has been painting canvases of her daughter, trying to create the perfect likeness. She sees Pallas with her infant son twice. Mavis's daughter Sally sees her mother in a diner and talks with her, and the two women apologize to one another. Seneca's mother Jean sees her in a parking lot, though Seneca says she does not remember her. Gigi, dressed in fatigues, and Pallas, carrying a sword, both seem prepared for battle when they appear to their parents. And Consolata reclines on a beach, her head in Piedade's lap. Piedade sings of solace while watching ships that bring the "disconsolate" to " . . . rest before shouldering the endless work they were created to do down here in Paradise" (318). The final vision suggests reincarnation and that Billie Delia's wish for the women to return will be fulfilled. Morrison has said that she intended the final word of the novel to be *paradise* with a lower-case "P" and has asked the publisher to make that correction in future printings. She said, "I wanted the book to be an interrogation of the idea of paradise and . . . to move it from its pedestal of exclusion and to make it more accessible to everybody" (Timehost).

The Novel's Reception

Morrison has said that she reads her reviews with interest and adds that " . . . the unflattering reviews are painful for short periods of time; the badly written ones are deeply, deeply insulting. That reviewer took no time to really read the book" (Jaffrey). As a former editor, she reads reviews from both a publisher's and a writer's perspective. Her novel *Paradise* was published to mixed reviews, partially because of readers' differing expectations. Some writers interpret the novel as allegory, while others look for realistic character development. While almost all reviewers praise the novel's lyricism, most also address the obscurity of the plot line, which many find unappealing. Readers agree on little else, presenting conflicting viewpoints of the novel's characterization, symbolism, themes, and politics. Indeed, most reviews are themselves somewhat conflicted, enthusiastically embracing some aspects of the novel while expressing reservations about others.

Louis Menand presents his own politics as a starting point for his discussion of the novel. He uses his review for *The New Yorker* as an opportunity to dispute the analysis of O.J. Simpson's murder trial Morrison puts forth in *Birth of a Nation'hood: Gaze, Script and Spectacle in the O.J. Simpson Case,* in which Morrison asserts her belief in Simpson's innocence. For Morrison, the presumption of Simpson's guilt is predicated on racist assumptions of the inherent violence and volatility of black masculinity. Despite its inauspicious beginning, Menand's is an intelligent and insightful review. He seems put off by the gender emphasis in the book, stating rather reductively that " . . . the male scapegoating of sexually unattached women . . . symbolize[s] the entire period of social bulence, from 1968 to 1976" (78). But he is respectful of Mo son's talent and calls *Paradise* her "strangest and most origi book" (78). He praises her subtle use of Biblical allusions and co pares the allegorical elements of the novel to some of Willia Faulkner's best work. For Menand, the difficulty of the narrative key to its method and the novel's power. Two of his criticisms o the novel are on-target, if arguable; he finds the magical ending forced, and he says "the lack of a central character is a liability that is never completely overcome" (81). That absence of a protagonist is, of course, intentional by Morrison; she wants readers to experience the town. While that strategy is demanding of readers, challenging her audience is something that the author has never avoided.

The story's gender politics is perhaps the most frequently discussed aspect of the novel. But when Morrison is asked if she agrees with the many reviewers who call *Paradise* a feminist novel, she rejects the label. She says that she wants to remain "as free as I possibly can, in my own imagination" and also points out that white male writers are not labeled the way that women and minority writers routinely are (Jaffrey). Morrison repeatedly attempts to distance herself from any labels, feeling that they are limiting and that they suggest that she sets out to do something programmatic. Gender conflicts are certainly at the heart of the story, however, so feminist analysis of the novel is appropriate. Nevertheless, those reviewers who focused on

gender as the novel's sole issue oversimplify both the novel's scope and the complexity of the town and characters.

The lyricism and sheer beauty of Morrison's language are routinely praised by reviewers, even those who did not like other aspects of the novel. Deidre Donahue of *USA Today*, for example, states that "no one writes as lushly as Toni Morrison" (1D). And John Kennedy, in *The Antioch Review*, calls her "rich, evocative and descriptive passages" "Faulknerian," though he thinks the chapter structure works against the novel's success. Reviewers likewise commend Morrison's apt sense of detail. Phil Baker, for example, reviewing the novel upon its paperback release for London's Sunday *Times*, says that "Morrison has peopled this microcosm of society with chillingly believable characters and coloured it in rich deep tones that enable the reader to feel the pitiless heat of the sun, smell the grits and coffee, and sense the tension in a passing glance."

In an unambivalently positive review, Peter Kemp praises exactly those qualities that other reviewers, as we will see below, dislike, showing that tastes vary widely. Kemp finds the characterizations complexly and realistically drawn, "brimming with all the energies and ambivalences of life . . . especially [the] contentments and bleaknesses at the heart of marriages." He praises her handling of the lasting violence of racism and the virtuosity of her employment of multiple narrative styles throughout the novel. For Kemp, *Paradise* is a masterful work of "psychological and social realism" that "doesn't only advocate respect, tolerance and generosity, it richly displays them."

Morrison's achievements as a writer, in addition to her Nobel Prize-winning status, pique readers' expectations. And her fame and status can encourage harshness in critics' appraisals. Michiko Katutani, for instance, wrote a scathing review for *The New York Times*. In addition to calling *Paradise* "heavy-handed" and "schematic," she says that it is " . . . a contrived formulaic book that mechanically pits men against women, old against young, the past against the present" (8). And she finds the characters undeveloped. She does, however, note that the novel develops many of the themes of *Beloved*, the earlier novel she clearly prefers. The review in the Sunday *Times* paints an entirely different picture. In a closer reading Brook Allen declares that *Paradise* " . . . is richly revelatory not only of human nature but of the troubled history of black America from Reconstruction through the civil rights movement." Allen reads *Paradise* as a symbolic novel, comparing its style to the works of Eugene O'Neill and Ralph Ellison. She feels that "the poetry, the emotion, [and] the broad symbolic plan" work together effectively, though the gender conflict strikes her as overdone (6).

Paradise's disrupted timeline and shifts in point-of-view alienated Marianne Wiggins, who reviewed the novel for the London *Times* and describes it as "lumbering" and "disjointed." Wiggins wanted the book to deal with the pioneer history of the American West and is disappointed by Morrison's setting the present of the novel in the "disco" years of the 1970s, which she calls "at best an insipid, and at worst a cowardly narrative choice." Also, for some reason, Wiggins senses that Morrison wants to move away from the subject of race, but is trapped by the subject matter for which she has become famous. What Wiggins acknowledges in the beginning of her review but seems to forget by the time she passes that judgment is that the history of the West *is* a history of peoples of different races and their relationships with one another. For Morrison or any novelist writing about the region to ignore racial issues would be to succumb to the mythology that plagued Americans' understanding for far too long, that of brave white pioneers fighting off savage Indians while dominating friendly ones.

Unlike Wiggins, Judy Doenges finds Morrison's use of multiple viewpoints "a masterful storytelling strategy that allows her to vividly highlight the crazy-quilt quality of rumor and history bred by mutual distrust." Doenges, writing for the Sunday edition of *The Seattle Times*, also praises the incorporation of magic that so many other reviewers criticize. She reads the novel as, among other things, an argument against separatism.

Colin Walters responds directly to Morrison's Nobel Prize-winning status in his review for *The Washington Times*. Walters seems to take offense at suggestions that Morrison "has given a new African-American and women's voice to literature" and to resent the comparison of her work to that of Faulkner, who also won the Nobel Prize for Literature. Walters prefers Morrison's earlier works, stating that her more recent novels "are too much dragged down by exaggerated effects and rhetorical overload" (B6). (One can only assume he fails to recognize the irony in that pronouncement; critics always preferred Faulkner's early novels and bemoaned the decline in his narrative powers. In more recent years, his later novels have received more attention and respect.) Ultimately, Walters's condemnation rests on Morrison's treatment of gender: "What disappoints . . . is Mrs. [sic] Morrison's valorizing of her women characters over her men, turning an otherwise engaging story . . . into a gothic gender war." While gender is certainly a major theme of the novel, Walters's reading ignores the many weaknesses in the book's female characters and the many strengths in its male ones.

Geoffrey Bent, in his review in the literary journal *The Southern Review*, seems to think that Morrison's goal was to describe an actual paradise when he calls *Paradise* "her weakest book." He faults "the didactic purity that underlies every paradise" and even suggests that the novel "can only send ripples of reappraisal back over the rest of her oeuvre" (145). Bent also feels that the massacre that begins the novel lacks sufficient motivation, and he finds the novel's symbolism heavy-handed. He seems to read the novel allegorically, as do most of the reviewers who fault Morrison's characterization. By contrast, Evelyn E. Shockley asserts that Morrison's "characters never stand in for a position; rather, each struggles to reconcile seemingly irreconcilable needs and desires" (718). Many reviewers, of course, praised the novel's characterization. Shockley's astute analysis of Morrison's method, however, helps to explain the discrepancies. She states that "Morrison's postmodern approach to language and narrative combines a poetic insistence upon the importance of every word with magical realism's freedom from linearity and representational constraints" (719). Paradoxically, the novel can be interpreted allegorically as well as realistically. While Morrison eschews the limited character development often associated with magical realism (a literary term used to describe fiction that incorporates magical or mystical events into an otherwise realistic narrative), her work nevertheless succeeds on the allegorical level even as it provides complex characterizations.

The most interesting reviews provide not just a plot summary and opinion but also questions for those who have read the novel. Elaine Kalman Naves, for instance, points out that the novel's epigraph and final sentence present contradictory moral schemas. The first admonishes against the sinful pleasures of earthly existence; the second suggests that life on earth is itself paradise. This and other contradictions in the novel prove challenging for readers. Naves's is a positive review of the novel, yet she notes that "despite its spiritual richness and complexity and its poetic and incantatory language, I felt distanced from its large cast of characters who often seem to be mouthpieces setting opposing political, historical and religious views." Like many reviewers, Naves also dislikes the mystical elements of the novel.

Of all the reviews, Gail Caldwell of *The Boston Globe* writes the cleverest opening sentence: "If my name were Evil, I'd watch my back around Toni Morrison, because she knows how to find the sunlight in a field of darkness and turn the rain to song." Caldwell's lighthearted beginning is fitting, because the seriousness of Morrison's subject matter often overshadows the abiding humor in her works. Caldwell focuses on the moral power of Morrison's works and likens her aesthetic command to that of William Faulkner, Virginia Woolf, and Gabriel García Márquez. She notes that Morrison documents "the inner journey of an entire town—the mythic archetypes of hubris and idealism and the curse of exclusion" and points out that "the dilapidated convent is both [Ruby's] mirror and its nemesis."

In addition to works by the authors noted above, *Paradise* has also been compared to Zora Neale Hurston's *Their Eyes Were Watching God*; both novels depict entire communities and confront skin-color biases among African Americans. Ron Charles makes this comparison in his review for *The Christian Science Monitor*. He points to racism as the underlying cause of the black town's demise. Charles also compares the Convent to the woman-centered community in Alice Walker's *The Color Purple*. However by limiting his commentary to issues of race and sex, he oversimplifies Morrison's complex novel. Judith Fitzgerald's review for *The Toronto Star* is similarly reductive, despite its elaborate praise, in its focus on the credibility of minor details and its summation of the novel's themes—"all human beings . . . will oppress the less fortunate among us." Ultimately, of course, readers are called on to determine their own conclusions on the novel and its meaning, and the resulting interpretations may well vary with each reading.

4

The Novel's Performance

The first novel after Morrison's Nobel Prize for Literature, *Paradise* was much anticipated. It had a first printing of 400,000 copies (Gray) and an abridged audio book narrated by Morrison herself was released in February 1998, just one month after the novel's appearance. *Paradise* was a Book-of-the-Month Club main selection and was also the second Morrison novel chosen by Oprah Winfrey for her talk show's enormously popular book club. The first was *Song of Solomon* (1977), which Winfrey picked in December 1996 as the second selection for her club. Morrison was unfamiliar with the book club at the time *Song of Solomon* was chosen, and she wondered "who's going to buy a book because of Oprah?" (Gray 68). When one million copies of the novel sold and sales of Morrison's other novels increased by approximately twenty-five percent, Morrison learned something about the power of television, and *The Oprah Winfrey Show* as well (Gray 68). Since then, in May 2000, *The Bluest Eye* also became an Oprah book club selection.

As part of her club, Winfrey invites the authors to discuss their work with readers from the audience who have been chosen based on letters they have written about how the book has affected them.

While the *Song of Solomon* show consisted of filmed portions of a discussion of the novel over a gourmet dinner for Morrison and just a few readers at Winfrey's home, the show on *Paradise* took a different format. It first aired on March 6, 1998. In addition to a one-on-one interview with Winfrey, the broadcast also showed part of a "class" of twenty-two people, led by Morrison for the winners of the letter-writing contest. This class was held at Princeton University, where Morrison is Robert Goheen Professor of the Humanities.

In the interview with Winfrey, Morrison explains that before writing the novel she conducted a great deal of research on the twenty-eight all-black towns established in Oklahoma. Twelve of those towns remain, and the show interviewed some of the citizens of two such towns, Langston and Rentiesville. Interviewees express abiding love for the towns, despite early hardships such as lack of a water supply. And they discussed the advantages of living in an all-black town with a special history. But they also mention disadvantages such as second-hand textbooks in the schools.

Morrison reports that she was surprised and pleased by the number of readers who read *Paradise* carefully, and one of the benefits of the show is the diverse opinions the participants offer. The discussion also gave the selected readers a chance to ask Morrison specific questions about their confusion. Winfrey reveals that four of her friends, while discussing their reading of the novel, became defensive about their *ability* to read because of its difficulty. Morrison responds that readers are not expected to understand everything on their first reading. Rather, she hopes for an intellectual response to the issues raised by the work on that initial reading. Readers should be cautioned not to try to reduce the novel to a simplified version of the text's philosophical questions, however, because Morrison has stated repeatedly that she does not write "issue" novels. She is not promoting a position but exploring problems that interest her and hopefully engage the reader. In addition to her interest in the nature of paradises and their exclusions, which Morrison has discussed in many of her interviews, she adds that she is interested in asking, "why is our imagination so weak when it comes to establishing it [paradise]." She notes that many of our descriptions of paradise sound like theme parks. She further emphasizes the status provided by the exclusion of others from such places. Morrison encourages the readers on the show to trust their understandings, even if they are having difficulty articulating them specifically. She clearly trusts both her readers and her work. Morrison also stresses that there is no central character in the novel because she "wanted to force the reader to become acquainted with the communities." She wants the experience of reading the novel to be akin to entering an unfamiliar town and getting to know the people. The disorientation that readers feel, then, is a crucial part of their experience.

One of the demands Morrison's fiction makes on its readers is that they sympathize with the characters, including the most faulted ones. An interesting story that Morrison relates on the show concerns her reaction to a reader who expressed anger at the meanness of Sal, Mavis's daughter. Morrison points out how difficult and frightening it would be to have Mavis as a mother. Mavis cannot defend herself against her abusive husband, Frank. And if she cannot protect herself, she cannot protect her children. As Morrison says, Sal knows that all the power lies with Frank. Mavis is incapable even of preparing a decent meal. Morrison also emphasizes that Sal would be afraid that she might grow up to be like Mavis. Her comments ask the reader who is angry at Sal to look at the situation from Sal's point-of-view in order to understand the motivation for her mean behavior to her mother.

Readers on the show wanted to know the races of the women at the Convent, which Morrison would not identify. She does discuss the critical functions of that first sentence—"They shoot the white girl first." It must "launch the story" and "seduce [the reader] im-

mediately into the narrative." The sentence also alerts readers that
race has a significant role in the text, though not the one to which
we are accustomed. The word *white* in that initial sentence does not
identify the race of a specific character. Rather, Morrison wanted it
"to signal race instantly and to reduce it to nothing." She adds that
it is difficult for the writer "to write race and to unwrite it at the same
time. So you have to withhold information." Readers respond differently to that sentence: Some try from that point to discover who
the white woman is, whereas others are far less concerned about the
racial identity. Morrison admits that she "wanted some strong response."

The question the readers on the show most wanted answered was
whether the Convent women are living or dead at the end of the novel.
One woman points out that the book refers to passages in Corinthians in the Bible and that the ending reminded her of the part of
Corinthians when Paul describes a paradise where it is not clear if
those in it are embodied or not. This paradise is a third place, in addition to earth and heaven; it is an "in-between" place. Morrison seems
pleased by this interpretation, nodding her head and smiling. She encourages the audience to think beyond either/or dichotomies, stating
that to ask if the women are living or dead is to "avoid the real question." The ending, she says, requires "being open to all these paths
and connections and interstices between." As evidenced by the book
reviews in the previous section, that demand proves too strenuous for
many readers, who are dissatisfied by the ending. The lack of speci-
ficity, however, does avoid the problem with descriptions of paradise
that Morrison mentions at the beginning of the *Oprah* show: that they
become static places that no longer hold our interest.

Oprah's book club can also be accessed electronically. There is
no longer an active chat group for the novel; however, the page for
Paradise has links to a short biography of Morrison, excerpts from
reviews of the novel, and discussion questions that can be used for

reading groups. Random House's site also provides such questions. *Suite101.com* provides a review of the novel as well as responses to that review and the opportunity to participate in the chat.

Paradise has attracted scholarly attention as well. Kristin Hunt's essay in *Reading Under the Sign of Nature: New Essays in Ecocriticism* applies W. E. B. DuBois's concept of double consciousness to an analysis of the role of the environment and geography in the novel. Hunt feels that the burden of double consciousness helps explain "a sense of restlessness experienced by black characters that can never be fully resolved; the characters are inherently limited in their quest for a sense of belonging and ultimately a connection to the land where they reside" (117). Double consciousness affects characters' relationships not only with each other but also to the environment. Hunt argues that Ruby's decline is signified by its citizens' losing their appreciation of the natural world. She posits the alienation from nature as the cause of Ruby's decline: "Ultimately it is the refusal to accept nature's course and to form bonds with the environment that brings about the demise of the clan's descendents" (122). That argument seems too extreme, however, as the causes of Ruby's failure as a community are many.

J. Brooks Bouson's more extensive interpretation of the novel is part of her study of the role of shame and trauma in Morrison's work. Of the Disallowing, Bouson asserts that "in a classic shame defense, Ruby's ancestors respond . . . with reactive pride." She connects this theme to "Morrison's persisting interest in the issues of intraracial shaming, the color-caste hierarchy, and the significance of shame and pride . . . in the construction of group identity" (196). Bouson compellingly connects the rejection suffered by Haven's settlers to their establishing their own caste system that favors darker skin; they thereby replicate "the rigid racial and economic demarcations and the polarizing binarisms of white/black and us/them found in the dominant culture" (197). Bouson also finds in the people's shame the source of their secrecy about their own lives. By contrast, the women at the Convent have been shamed but come to discover, through Consolata Sosa, the transformed Connie, "the beloved or divine part of the self" (211).

While *Paradise* has engendered various conflicting and passionate responses and its place in Morrison's canon will no doubt continue to be debated, it is clearly a rich source for study and discussion. Infused not only with racial and gender tensions but also with the conflict between the demands of community and individual freedom that are constitutive of American identity, it will continue to be an enlightening resource for its readers.

5

Further Reading and Discussion Questions

1. How do Haven and Ruby compare with other accounts of utopias or paradises?

2. Morrison has lamented the poverty of imagination underlying most descriptions of paradise. How would you describe paradise? What kind of community would you like to create, or what is one thing you would like to change about your present community?

3. Morrison has said that she wanted to explore why concepts of paradise are always based on exclusion. What other social or cultural institutions can you think of that are based on exclusion? What purpose does the exclusion serve? Is such exclusivity necessarily negative or harmful? When is or isn't it?

4. Discuss the relationships among the women at the Convent. Why are Mavis and Gigi so antagonistic?

5. Mavis, Gigi, Seneca, and Pallas all witness or experience violence. What is similar about their experiences of violence and their reactions to it? What do all the violent stories add to the novel as a whole? What characters in Ruby experience similar violence?

6. How does Soane and Deacon's marriage compare with Dovey and Steward's? How are those marriages different from the others

described in the book, such as K.D. and Arnette's or Pat Best and Billy Cato's? How do the town's characteristics affect the marriages?

7. At different times, Sweetie, Arnette, Billie Delia, and Menus all seek refuge at the Convent, and each of them is cared for there. What leads them to seek help there? How do they respond to the help and relate to the Convent after they leave? What accounts for their different reactions?

8. Connie avoids direct light as much as possible, making her bedroom in the cellar and constantly wearing sunglasses. What does her aversion to light signify?

9. How do the mystical events in the novel, such as Zachariah's vision and Connie's power, affect your reading of the story?

10. The stories behind the founding of Haven become powerful myths for the people of Ruby. What myths—or stories that are repeated again and again—exist in your own family and community, and what purpose do they serve? What aspects of the stories are exaggerated?

11. The novel presents very little interaction between parents and children. What do we know of parent–child relationships in Ruby?

12. Discuss the differences between Deacon and Steward. What distinguishes these twins who are so much alike earlier in the novel? What accounts for their different reactions at the end?

13. What do Deek and Connie learn from their affair? How do they reinterpret the meaning of the affair at the end of the novel?

14. Lone is introduced late in the novel. What new perspective toward Ruby does she add? What new information do we find out about the residents from her? What do you make of her relationship with Connie?

15. Connie is at first very suspicious of Lone's magic, and she feels guilty for using her resurrecting powers because she thinks doing so is a sin. How do you feel about her changed attitude?

Should we be as suspicious of her conversion as we have become of other religious practices in the novel?

16. How do you interpret the end of the novel? Have the Convent women been resurrected? Are we supposed to believe that they will return to Earth, and if so, to what purpose? How is the impression we get of the women's family members different in these last scenes than earlier in the book?

17. Piedade seems very important at the end of the novel, yet we are given very little information about her. Do you think she is a divinity, and if so, what kind?

18. One of the challenges of making a film version of *Beloved* was portraying the novel's magical elements visually. If you were going to make a film of *Paradise*, how would you portray its magical elements? Who would you cast in lead roles?

19. If you had the opportunity to interview Morrison, what would you ask?

20. How do the themes in *Paradise* relate to those in other works by Morrison that you have read? How does the novel compare with books by other authors?

Further Reading
Works by Other Authors with Similar Styles or Themes

Bambara, Toni Cade. *Those Bones Are Not My Child.* New York: Vintage, 2000.

Butler, Octavia. *Kindred.* Boston: Beacon, 1988.

Carey, Peter. *Bliss.* New York: Random House, 1996.

———. *Oscar and Lucinda.* New York: Vintage, 1997.

———. *True History of the Kelly Gang.* New York: Knopf, 2001.

Danticat, Edwidge. *Breath, Eyes, Memory.* New York: Vintage, 1995.

Faulkner, William. *The Sound and the Fury.* 1929. *The Corrected Text.* New York: Vintage, 1990.

——. *As I Lay Dying*. 1930. *The Corrected Text*. New York: Vintage, 1990.

——. *Absalom, Absalom!* 1936. New York: Vintage, 1990.

——. *Go Down, Moses*. 1942. New York: Vintage, 1990

García-Márquez, Gabriel. *Chronicle of a Death Foretold*. Trans. Gregory Rabassa. New York: Knopf, 1983.

——. *One Hundred Years of Solitude*. Trans. Gregory Rabassa. New York: Harper Perennial, 1991.

——. *Love in the Time of Cholera*. Trans. Edith Grossman. New York: Viking Penguin, 1999.

Harris, Middleton, ed. *The Black Book*. New York: Random House, 1974.

Hurston, Zora Neale. *Their Eyes Were Watching God*. Urbana: University of Illinois Press, 1978.

Kincaid, Jamaica. *Annie John*. New York: New American Library, 1986.

——. *Lucy*. Farrar, Straus & Giroux, 1990.

——. *The Autobiography of My Mother*. Farrar, Straus & Giroux, 1996.

Naylor, Gloria. *The Women of Brewster Place*. New York: Penguin, 1982.

——. *Linden Hills*. New York: Penguin, 1985.

——. *Mama Day*. New York: Vintage, 1988.

——. *Bailey's Cafe*. New York: Vintage, 1992.

Pynchon, Thomas. *The Crying of Lot 49*. New York: Harper and Row, 1966.

——. *Vineland*. 1990. New York: Penguin, 1997.

——. *Mason & Dixon*. New York: Holt, 1998.

Shields, Carol. *The Stone Diaries*. New York: Viking, 1995.

——. *Small Ceremonies*. New York: Viking, 1995.

Walker, Alice. *Meridian*. New York: Pocket, 1976.

——. *The Color Purple*. New York: Pocket, 1982.

——. *The Temple of My Familiar*. New York: Pocket, 1989.

——. *Possessing the Secret of Joy*. New York: Harcourt Brace Jovanovich, 1992.

Works Written or Edited by Toni Morrison

Beloved. New York: Knopf, 1987.

The Big Box. With Slade Morrison. Illus. Giselle Potter. New York: Jump at the Sun, 1999.

Birth of a Nation'hood: Gaze, Script, and Spectacle in the O.J. Simpson Case, Ed. with Claudia Brodsky Lacour. New York: Pantheon, 1997.

The Black Book, ed. compiled by Middleton Harris, with the assistance of Morris Levitt, Roger Furman, Ernest Smith. New York: Random House, 1974.

The Bluest Eye. New York: Holt, 1970.

"City Limits, Village Values: Concepts of the Neighborhood in Black Fiction." *Literature and the Urban Experience: Essays on the City and Literature*. Ed. Michael Jaye and Ann Watts. New Brunswick: Rutgers UP, 1981, 35–43.

The Dancing Mind: Speech upon Acceptance of the National Book Foundation Medal for Distinguished Contribution to American Letters on the Sixth of November, Nineteen Hundred and Ninety-Six. New York: Knopf, 2000.

"Home." *The House That Race Built*. Ed. Wahneema Lubiano. New York: Vintage, 1998.

Honey and Rue. Lyrics. Musical score by André Previn. 1992.

Jazz. New York: Knopf, 1992.

"On the Backs of Blacks." *Arguing Immigration: The Debate Over the Changing Face of America*. Ed. Nicolaus Mills. New York: Touchstone, 1994.

Paradise. New York: Knopf, 1998.

Playing in the Dark: Whiteness and the Literary Imagination. New York: Vintage, 1993.

Race-ing Justice, En-gendering Power: Essays on Anita Hill, Clarence Thomas, and the Construction of Social Reality, ed. New York: Pantheon, 1992.

"Recitatif." *Confirmation: An Anthology of African American Women*. Eds. Amiri Baraka (LeRoi Jones) and Amina Baraka. New York: William Morrow, 1983, 243–261.

"Rootedness: The Ancestor as Foundation." *Black Women Writers (1950–1980): A Critical Evaluation*. Ed. Mari Evans. Garden City, NY: Anchor/Doubleday, 1983. 339–45.

"The Site of Memory." *Inventing the Truth: The Art and Craft of Memoir*. Ed. William Zinsser. Boston: Houghton Mifflin, 1987, 103–24.

Song of Solomon. New York: Knopf, 1977.

Sula. New York: Knopf, 1973.

Tar Baby. New York: Knopf, 1981.

"Unspeakable Things Unspoken: The Afro-American Presence in American Literature." *Michigan Quarterly Review* 38 (1989): 1—34.

Interviews

Borders.com. "A Conversation with Toni Morrison." http://www.borders .com/features/MMK98004.html.

Brown, Cecil. "Interview with Toni Morrison." *The Massachusetts Review* 36.3 (1995): 455–73.

Darling, Marsha. "In the Realm of Responsibility: A Conversation with Toni Morrison." *Women's Review of Books*, March 1988: 5–6.

Donahue, Deirdre. "Morrison's Slice of Paradise." *USA Today Books*, Jan. 8, 1998. http://www.usatoday.com/life/enter/books/b128.htm.

Dreifus, Claudiea. "Chloe Wofford Talks about Toni Morrison." *New York Times Magazine* Sept. 11, 1994, 72–75.

Farnsworth, Elizabeth. "Conversation: Toni Morrison." *The NewsHour with Jim Lehrer Transcript.* March 9, 1998. http://www.pbs.org/newshour/bb/ entertainment/jan-june98/morrison_3-9.html.

Gilroy, Paul. "Living Memory: A Meeting with Toni Morrison." *Small Acts: Thoughts on the Politics of Black Cultures.* London: Serpent's Tail, 1993. 175–82.

Jaffrey, Zia. "Toni Morrison: The Salon Interview." *Salon.* Feb. 2, 1998. http://www.salon.com/books/int/1998/02/cov_si_02int.html

LeClair, Thomas. "The Language Must Not Sweat." *New Republic*, March 1981: 25–29.

Micucci, Dana. "An Inspired Life: Toni Morrison Writes and a Generation Listens." *Conversations with Toni Morrison.* Ed. Danille Taylor-Guthrie. Jackson: University Press of Mississippi, 1994, 275–279.

Naylor, Gloria. "A Conversation: Gloria Naylor and Toni Morrison." *The Southern Review*, 21 (1985): 567–93.

Ruas, Charles. Toni Morrison. *Conversations with Toni Morrison.* Ed. Danille Taylor-Guthrie. Jackson: University Press of Mississippi, 1994, 93–118.

Schappell, Elissa, with Lacour, Claudia Brodskey. "Toni Morrison: The Art of Fiction CXXXIV." *The Paris Review*, 35. 128 (1993): 82–125.

Stepto, Robert. "Intimate Things in Place: A Conversation with Toni Morrison." *Conversations with Toni Morrison.* Ed. Danille Taylor-Guthrie. Jackson: University Press of Mississippi, 1994. 10–29.

Taylor-Guthrie, Danille, ed. *Conversations with Toni Morrison.* Jackson: University Press of Mississippi, 1994.

Wilson, Judith. "A Conversation with Toni Morrison." *Essence,* July 1981: 84–86, 128–134.

Winfrey, Oprah. *The Oprah Winfrey Show.* March 6, 1998.

Web Sites

"Paradise." Oprah Book Club site. http://www.oprah.com/obc/pastbooks/toni_morrison/obc_pb_19980116_a.html.

Powers, Robert. Review of Paradise. *Suite 101.com.* http://www.i5ive.com/article.cfm/new_books/5171 Site provides chat space related to the article.

Random House's *Paradise* site. http://www.randomhouse.com/features/paradise/paradise. Has link to a reading group guide with questions about the novel.

"Timehost Chat." *Time.com.* Jan. 21, 1998. http://www.time.com/time/community/transcripts/chattr012198.html.

"Toni Morrison AOL Live Chat." May 25, 2000. http://www.oprah.com/com/chat/transcript/obc/chat_trans_tmorrison.html.

Toni Morrison Society. http://www.gsu.edu/~wwwtms.

Reviews of *Paradise*

Allen, Brooke. "The Promised Land." *The New York Times* Jan. 11, 1998: 6.

Baker, Phil. "*Paradise* by Toni Morrison." *The Times* (London) April 4, 1999.

Bent, Geoffrey. "Less Than Divine: Toni Morrison's *Paradise.*" *The Southern Review* 35 (1999): 145–49.

Caldwell, Gail. "West of Eden: Toni Morrison's Shimmering Story of an Oklahoma Paradise That's Asking for Trouble." *The Boston Globe,* Jan. 11, 1998: F1.

Charles, Ron. "Toni Morrison's Feminist Portrayal of Racism." *The Christian Science Monitor,* Jan. 29, 1998: B1.

Donahue, Deirdre. "Morrison Presents a Profound *Paradise*." *USA Today*, Jan. 8, 1998: 1D.

Fitzgerald, Judith. "Woes Aplenty in this *Paradise*." *The Toronto Star*, Jan. 31, 1998: M15.

Kakutani, Michiko. "Worthy Women, Unredeemable Men." *The New York Times*, Jan. 6, 1998: 8.

Kemp, Peter. "Sacred and Profane." *Sunday Times*, March 22, 1998.

Kennedy, John. Review of Paradise. *Antioch Review*, 58 (2000): 377.

Mulrine, Anna. "This Side of *Paradise*: Toni Morrison Defends Herself from Criticism of Her New Novel." *U. S. News and World Report*, Jan. 19, 1998. Available *U. S. News Online*. http://www.usnews.com/usnews/issue/980119/19new.htm.

Menand, Louis. "The War Between Men and Women." *The New Yorker*, Jan. 12, 1998: 78–82.

Naves, Elaine Kalman. "The American Experience, Edged in Black." *The Gazette (Montreal)* Feb. 14, 1998: J1.

Shockley, Evelyn E. Review of *Paradise*. *African American Review* 33 (1999): 718–719.

Walters, Colin. "This Nobel Laureate's *Paradise* Is Lost." *The Washington Times*, Jan. 25, 1998: B6.

Wiggins, Marianne. "No Winner in This Race." *The Times*, March 19, 1998.

Books and Articles on African-Americans in the West

Crockett, Norman. *The Black Towns*. Lawrence: Regents Press of Kansas, 1979.

Franklin, Jimmie Lewis. *Journey Toward Hope: A History of Blacks in Oklahoma*. Norman: University of Oklahoma Press, 1982.

Glasrud, Bruce A. *African-Americans in the West: A Bibliography of Secondary Sources*. Center for Big Bend Studies Occasional Papers, No. 2. Alpine, Texas: Sul Ross State University, 1998.

Katz, William Loren. *Black People Who Made the Old West*. Trenton, NJ: Africa World Press, 1992.

———. *The Black West*. Rev. ed. Garden City, NY: Anchor, 1973.

Ravage, John W. *Black Pioneers: Images of the Black Experience on the North American Frontier.* Salt Lake City: University of Utah Press, 1997.

Taylor, Quintard. *In Search of the Racial Frontier: African-Americans in the American West, 1528–1990.* New York: Norton, 1998.

Related Secondary Sources

Awkward, Michael. *Inspiriting Influences: Tradition, Revision, and African-American Women's Novels.* New York: Columbia University Press, 1989.

Bjork, Patrick. *The Novels of Toni Morrison: The Search for Self and Place Within the Community.* New York: Lang, 1992.

Bloom, Harold, ed. *Toni Morrison: Modern Critical Views.* New York: Chelsea House, 1990.

Bouson, J. Brooks. *Quiet As It's Kept: Shame, Trauma, and Race in the Novels of Toni Morrison.* Albany: State University of New York Press, 2000.

Carmean, Karen. *Toni Morrison's World of Fiction.* Troy, New York: Whitston Publishing, 1993.

Christian, Barbara. *Black Women Novelists: The Development of a Tradition, 1892–1976.* Westport: Greenwood, 1980.

Cozzens, Lisa. "The Civil Rights Movement 1955–1965." *African American History.* http://fledge.watson.org/~lisa/ blackhistory/civilrights-55-65. May 25, 1998.

David, Ron. *Toni Morrison Explained: A Reader's Road Map to the Novels.* New York: Random House, 2000.

Davis, Angela. *Women, Race and Class.* New York: Random House, 1981.

Furman, Jan. *Toni Morrison's Fiction.* Columbia: University of South Carolina Press, 1996.

Gates, Henry Louis, Jr., and Appiah, K. Anthony, eds. *Toni Morrison: Critical Perspectives Past and Present.* New York: Amistad, 1993.

Gray, Paul. "Paradise Found." *Time,* Jan 19, 1998: 62–68.

Harris, Trudier. *Exorcising Blackness: Historical and Literary Lynching and Burning Rituals.* Bloomington: Indiana University Press, 1984.

———. *Fiction and Folklore: The Novels of Toni Morrison.* Knoxville: University of Tennessee Press, 1991.

———. "Toni Morrison." *The Oxford Companion to Women's Writing in the United States*. Ed. Cathy N. Davidson and Linda Wagner-Martin. New York: Oxford UP, 1995. 578–580.

Heinze, Denise. *The Dilemma of "Double-Consciousness": Toni Morrison's Novels*. Athens: University of Georgia Press, 1993.

Holloway, Karla F. C. *Moorings and Metaphors: Figures of Culture and Gender in Black Women's Literature*. New Brunswick, New Jersey: Rutgers University Press, 1992.

———. *Codes of Conduct: Race, Ethics, and the Color of Our Character*. New Brunswick, New Jersey: Rutgers UP, 1995.

Holloway, Karla F. C. and Demetrakopoulos, Stephanie A. *New Dimensions of Spirituality: A Biracial and Bicultural Reading of the Novels of Toni Morrison*. New York: Greenwood, 1987

hooks, bell. *Black Looks: Race and Representation*. Boston: South End, 1981.

Hunt, Kristin. "Paradise Lost: The Destructive Forces of Double Consciousness and Boundaries in Toni Morrison's *Paradise*." *Reading Under the Sign of Nature: New Essays in Ecocriticism*. Eds. John Tallmadge and Henry Harrington. Salt Lake City: University of Utah Press, 2000.

Jones, Bessie W., and Vinson, Audrey L. *The World of Toni Morrison: Explorations in Literary Criticism*. Dubuque: Kendall/Hunt, 1985.

Kolmerten, Carol A., Ross, Stephen M., and Wittenberg, Judith Bryant. *Unflinching Gaze: Morrison and Faulkner Re-Envisioned*. Jackson: University Press of Mississippi, 1997.

Kubitschek, Missy Dehn. *Toni Morrison: A Critical Companion*. Westport, Connecticut: Greenwood, 1998.

Matus, Jill. *Toni Morrison*. Manchester: Manchester University Press, 1998.

Mbalia, Doreatha Drummond. *Toni Morrison's Developing Class Consciousness*. Selingsgrove: Susquehanna University Press, 1991.

McKay, Nellie Y. *Critical Essays on Toni Morrison*. Boston: G. K. Hall, 1988.

Middleton, David L., ed. *Toni Morrison's Fiction: Contemporary Criticism*. New York: Garland, 1997.

Otten, Terry. *The Crime of Innocence in Toni Morrison's Fiction*. Columbia: University of Missouri Press, 1989.

Page, Philip. *Dangerous Freedom: Fusion and Fragmentation in Toni Morrison's Novels.* Jackson: University of Mississippi Press, 1995.

Peach, Linda. *Toni Morrison.* 2nd ed. New York: St. Martin's, 2000.

——. *Toni Morrison: Contemporary Critical Essays.* London: Macmillan, 1998.

Rigney, Barbara. *The Voices of Toni Morrison.* Columbus: Ohio State University Press, 1991.

Samuels, Wilfred D. and Hudson-Weems, Clenora. *Toni Morrison.* Boston: Twayne, 1990.

Wall, Cheryl, ed. *Changing Our Own Words: Essays on Criticism, Theory, and Writing by Black Women.* New Brunswick: Rutgers University Press, 1989.

Weinstein, Philip M. *What Else But Love? The Ordeal of Race in Faulkner and Morrison.* New York: Columbia, 1996.